RELATIONSHIP
ALCHEMY

DRAGON PRESS

Copyright ©2025 Joey Klein
All rights reserved.

No part of this publication may be reproduced or transmitted in any form or by any means, electronic or mechanical, including photography, recording, or any information storage and retrieval system, without permission in writing from the author. Requests for permission to make copies of any part of the work should be emailed to the following address: caitlynfagan@joeyklein.com.

Neither the publisher nor the author shall be liable for any loss of profit or any other commercial damages, including but not limited to special, incidental, consequential, personal, or other damages.

Published and distributed by Dragon Press, LLC.
Littleton, Colorado, USA

Library of Congress Control Number: 2025902765
Klein, Joey
Relationship Alchemy: A Practical Guide to Getting Along Well With Others

ISBN
Paperback 979-8-9924754-0-1
Hardcover 979-8-9924754-2-5
eBook 979-8-9924754-1-8

RELATIONSHIP ALCHEMY

A PRACTICAL GUIDE TO GETTING
ALONG WELL WITH OTHERS

JOEY KLEIN

CONTENTS

Resources		3
Foreword		5
Introduction		9
Why Are You Reading This Book?		19
1	It Starts with a Vision	31
2	Your Alignment with Vision	51
3	Emotions and Accountability	67
4	Setting Expectations for Yourself	91
5	Understanding the Relationship	107
6	Defining Boundaries	117
7	Communication	127
8	Sabotaging and Saving the Relationship	141
9	Know the Other Person	157
10	Expectations and the Other Person	169
11	Expectation Challenges	181
12	Vision and the Other Person	189
13	Vibrant Routines	201
14	My Hope for You	207
Acknowledgements		210
Inner Matrix Systems Membership		212
Elite Cohort		214
1:1 Mastery Training		216
Speaking		218
The Inner Matrix		220
About The Author		222

For all the relationships that have shaped me—those that challenged, nurtured, or inspired me—and to the clients who trusted me with theirs. To Caitlyn, who supports me in everything, always. And to the relationships yet to come, may they grow, transform, and thrive with the insights shared in these pages.

RESOURCES

A cornerstone of having vibrant relationships is developing our capacity to manage our side of the relationship, which includes managing ourselves emotionally and mentally. If you do not feel equipped to manage your state, we've got you. Inner Matrix Systems (www.innermatrixsystems.com/power_series) teaches a foundational curriculum, the Power Series, that trains people all over the world to develop and master themselves, and create lives better than they imagined possible.

POWER OF EMOTION

If you find yourself caught in anxiety, sadness, or anger and find it difficult to stay centered, please jump into Power of Emotion to develop your emotional intelligence and acuity. Master your emotions, and you'll master not only your relationships, but your life.

POWER OF FOCUS

If you notice that you get caught in the criticism of others, or if you struggle with skills like active listening, Power of Focus supports you to focus and direct the mind. This course helps you master the art of mindset training so the mind will no longer keep you from the fulfilling relationships you could have.

POWER OF VISION

If you struggle to clearly name your vision for relationships, check out Power of Vision. Vision is a skill that isn't taught at home or at school. In order to name and create vision, you need a framework and training in how to use it.

POWER OF INTUITION

Finally, if you are unsure how to move forward and don't know what to focus on first, Power of Intuition supports you to develop and leverage the skill of intuition. Intuition bridges the gap between where you are and where you want to go.

Remember, your relationships cannot grow beyond you. The more you grow within yourself, the better you get at managing that first aspect of a relationship, the more it will translate into fulfillment in your relationships and in your life.

Visit JoeyKlein.com, email admin@joeyklein.com, or call us at 720-446-5533 for more information and a complimentary training.

> **MAGNIFICENT, VIBRANT RELATIONSHIPS ARE AT THE HEART OF LIVING A FULFILLING LIFE, AND YOU DESERVE TO HAVE THEM. THE POWER SERIES CURRICULUM IS HERE TO HELP YOU DO JUST THAT.**

FOREWORD

WELCOME TO *RELATIONSHIP ALCHEMY!*

In 2019, I sat in on a weekend intensive with Joey Klein entitled "Vibrant Relationships." I was captivated by his depth of knowledge and inspiring style of delivering practical tools and deeply wise concepts within an incredibly powerful system designed to transform any relationship. During that weekend, I sincerely wished that everyone I knew, everyone I cared about, was at that program.

Joey's tools, techniques, and strategies are perfectly suited for all types of relationships: romantic partners, friendships, relationships with parents, relationships with children, and business partnerships. At lunch one day in early 2021, I urged Joey to write a book for couples and parents. I am grateful that he devoted his time and expertise to make this book available to us all.

I, myself, have been a licensed marriage and family therapist for more than thirty-five years and a licensed clinical psychologist for more than thirty-one years. I have been impressed with how Joey's system integrates the best of neurobiology and psychology to create more loving, respectful, and fulfilling relationships than most people thought possible. I have spent the last five years learning and training the emotional tools and thought strategies described in this book. As a direct result, my own marriage of twenty years has grown more deeply loving, more playful, more joyful, and more satisfying.

Relationships are an imperative aspect of our everyday lives, whether it's interacting with family, romantic partners, business partners, tellers at the bank, food service individuals, teachers, or grocery clerks.

On more than one occasion, I have observed a person lose their composure toward someone who was doing the best they could at their job. The enraged individual probably has no idea what impact they are having on the other person and those around the scene. If they think they have an idea of the impact they are having, they are most likely wrong. Instead of them controlling the situation, their emotions are in control of them. Sadly, it's highly likely that this is how they show up in many relationships in their lives.

Most people do not fully understand the impact their emotions, thoughts, and actions have on others—at least not in the way that Joey illustrates it. At the core of this book are the tools to empower you to create the quality relationships you desire. With proper implementation, the toolkit you have in your hands for everyday emotional mastery will enable you to influence the relationships in your life for the better.

Emotional intelligence translates to relationship intelligence. Relationship intelligence predicts success in one's personal as well as professional life. The principles discussed in this book apply to friendships, family members, your children, coworkers, your boss, and your customers. You're going to see how to create a new confidence and experience of fulfillment that can completely redefine how you see and interact with the people in your lives.

In this book, you will do a deep dive to construct a crystal-clear understanding of your vision for your life and the relationships you desire. You will be exploring areas of physical intimacy, emotional intimacy, sex, dating, parenting, family, health, lifestyle, and finances. Throughout each of these topics, you will be guided to construct a clear understanding of what is imperative to you in your relationships, how to communicate that clearly and specifically, how to confirm that the other person understands, and whether they are willing to show up for you. This book will enable you to further develop your capacity in all areas of your relationships.

Joey Klein has spent the last two decades dedicated to training people how to experience a life greater than they ever dreamed possible. He has spent more than a decade studying with world-class psychologists, philosophers, and neuroscientists to combine the best of the best in his system. I have experienced the truth that the tools, techniques, and strategies in this book really do work!

If you desire to be a creator in your life, enabling more deeply connected, mutually satisfying, and fulfilling relationships, you have found the perfect starting place!

LYDIA GLASS, PH.D.

INTRODUCTION

YOUR RELATIONSHIP IS 100% YOU,
NOT 50% YOU. THAT'S OWNERSHIP.

"Where is it?" My long-distance girlfriend's accusatory eyes scanned my Los Angeles home. I stood in shock. This was not a new pattern in our relationship, yet I still felt unprepared. "This picture usually sits here, and it's all the way over there!" she yelled. "Why was it moved? Did you put this in the drawer and take it back out? Do you put this away when I'm gone?"

I could feel her anxious and frightened energy build, while frustration began to rise inside of me.

"I don't know why it's moved," I responded, suddenly realizing that my girlfriend had strategically placed photos of us around my home as some kind of test of trust. "I don't clean this place—I don't have time. My cleaning person probably moved it. She likely picked it up, wiped it, and then put it back down. I didn't realize it was supposed to go exactly there!"

As her eyes burned into me, I could tell that she didn't believe me, even though everything I said was true. I felt myself reaching my limit. "Are you crazy?" I yelled. I immediately regretted both my tone and choice of words. It was a terrible response, but I didn't know what else to say in the face of these baseless accusations.

Within just forty-five minutes of arriving at my home, she grabbed her bags and left. I felt no desire to follow, chase after her, or beg for her forgiveness this time. I was done. This incident was a new level of mistrust between us, but it was perfectly in line with the recurring pattern that had defined our relationship from the start.

Perhaps you've found yourself in a similar situation.

HOW IT STARTED

I liked this woman. She was smart, charismatic, and beautiful. We seemed to have a great spark right from the start, and I was excited to give our long-distance relationship a try. I took it as a healthy sign of vulnerability when she shared early on that she was a bit insecure. She said to me, "I need you to help me with my insecurity."

As someone who likes to figure things out and succeed, I thought to myself, "Great! Let's fix this!" I was game to do whatever she needed to help her feel safe and confident in our relationship. I knew from past experiences that safety was a basic and important need, so it became my personal mission to help her.

When she asked me to call her every day for a check-in, I agreed. I even put a reminder on my calendar to ensure I upheld my promise to be a good boyfriend and call her whenever I had a break from my busy work and martial arts training schedule. Sometimes the calls came in the morning. Sometimes they were midday. On my really hectic days, I wouldn't get around to calling until the evening. But I called every single day, just as she had asked.

It only took a week to see that calling daily was not enough to make her feel secure. She started asking questions like, "Why did you call me in the afternoon instead of the evening?" I would reply, "That's when I had time." Then she'd say, "Well, what did you do last night? I think it's better if you call me before bed."

Trying to be a good boyfriend, I complied. "Okay, I can do that." But then I realized the plan didn't actually work with my schedule. Some nights I wouldn't get home from training at the dojang until 11 p.m. I would struggle with the decision of either calling her and possibly waking her up or not calling and causing her to feel that something was wrong.

I shared my concern with her, and she asked me to call her regardless of the time. So, on those late nights, bone-tired from a long day, I would still call only to be met with, "Why are you calling me so late? Who was there? Did she just leave?"

I was shocked. What was happening? Was I seriously being accused of cheating after an exhausting day of working and training? She knew my schedule. I barely had time to relax, let alone have another relationship. I thought I had been showing up for her the way she needed, yet it still wasn't enough.

Did I throw in the towel? No. She asked me to work harder to help her overcome her insecurity, and I did. I really wanted this relationship to work, and I wanted to be the hero who could save her. Daily calls turned into multiple calls per day. The more I played along, the more I fueled the pattern. Her requests weren't coming from a place of, "I love you and want to connect." They were coming from an insecure place. If I could have read her mind, it might have said, "I really want to trust you, but I don't. So, I am going to watch you closely until your actions begin to permit me to try and trust you."

In our relationship, she was laser-focused on what she feared most—betrayal. She searched for evidence of it in every conversation and interaction. If you've ever heard the phrase, "Where your intention goes, your energy flows," you won't be surprised that her actions and my reactions only increased her feelings of insecurity. The more attention we gave it, the worse it became, eventually culminating in that moment in my apartment with her analyzing the placement of photos.

Was her departure to the airport that day the end of it? Of course not! She called me from the airport asking, "Aren't you going to call me?" This time, I stood my ground. I reminded her that she said she was done with us and was leaving. She became more upset and said, "You're just going to let me leave?" She asked me to come pick her up from the airport. I told her she could find her way back if she wanted to. She hung up.

Were we done then? (You know the answer by now.)

She called me back, and the same loop continued—another threat to leave, followed by the expectation that I would chase her and bend over backward to prove my devotion. I didn't shut the door on our relationship, but for the first time, I drew a line. If she wanted to give this relationship another try, she would have to take action and come back to me. My chasing and fawning were done.

That relationship ended poorly.

CAN YOU RELATE?

Have you ever been in a relationship in which someone made you responsible for their emotional state? Or have you blamed your own emotional state on another person's words, actions, or behaviors?

That relationship with my ex-girlfriend was an eye-opening moment for me. I realized that, despite how much I cared for her and all her good qualities, there was nothing I could do to change her insecurity for her. Even if I *wanted* to fix it, which I did, there was no way I could. It was a difficult realization to face, but it was also freeing. I was no longer responsible for managing another person's emotions.

To clarify, I'm not saying our behaviors *don't* influence others. In fact, one of the goals of this book is to help you understand how managing your emotional state can lead to positive changes in your relationships. You cannot force someone else to change, nor can you manipulate them into doing so. However, you can positively influence how people in your life respond to you. That's an important distinction.

In my own life, I realized that my relationships followed a repeating pattern—they were chaotic. I grew up in a challenging household where interactions alternated between screaming matches and moments of distance and disconnection. From a young age, I had a sense that relationships could (and should) be different, but being surrounded by chaos for so long made that environment feel like home.

At the same time, I had an awareness of this pre-programmed track I seemed to be on. If I didn't learn to change, my relationships as an adult would likely follow the same patterns as those of my youth. As I matured, I became obsessed with learning a new way of living.

My search took me around the world, collecting lessons along the way. I found wisdom in unlikely places—from a dojo in Andover, Kansas, where I earned my black belt in Okinawan-Kenpo, to working with a best-selling self-help author in Boulder, Colorado. I studied at an ashram in Varanasi, India with an Indian guru who had lived in a cave for eight years, and I trained privately with one of Beverly Hills' most prominent clinical psychologists, Dr. LaWanda Katzman Staenberg (Dr. Lu).

My younger self would be shocked to know that, as an adult, I have educated thousands of people around the world on how to build more vibrant relationships. My younger self would never believe that the desperate childhood years of being beaten on by my older brothers would eventually transform me into a three-time world champion in Hwa Rang Do as well as a speaker at the 2005 United Nations International Peace Summit. In my early 20s, I had a near-death experience due to abusing substances to escape reality. Today my life is filled with health, authentic love, and connection—a life in which I *want* to be present because of how incredible it is.

This extreme transformation in my life isn't to brag; it's to show you that change is absolutely possible if 1) we choose to change, and 2) we take the right actions to make it happen. It takes both desire and movement in the direction of our vision. Without both components, wishing for a relationship change is about as helpful as wishing to be physically fit. The desire is not enough. You can't just read books on weightlifting and hope to get nice biceps (unless, of course, those books are especially heavy and you do curls with them while you read). You can't change your relationships and your life without a clear vision of what you want and an action plan that moves you in that direction.

Let's normalize reinvention in our lives and give ourselves permission to change and grow—at any age, in any relationship, over and over again.

RELATIONSHIPS ARE IMPERATIVES

While the idea of escaping society to live in a cave like the guru from the ashram may seem appealing to some, the reality is that relationships are a necessary part of our lives. However, most relationships we form aren't created with conscious intention. More often than not, our relationships are determined simply by who happened to be around at certain points in our lives.

Think about that. How did you meet your significant other? How did you meet your friends? Were they the people you went to school with? Did you meet at work? Were they your neighbors or people you met through a sport or activity?

If you take a look at your life, you'll probably find that most of the people in it are those who just happened to be there. On the other hand, there may be some relationships you designed and cultivated with due diligence on the front end. You may have had a clear vision of the romantic partner you wanted based on values and a vision of life you shared, or the business partner you found that shared similar principles and work ethic.

How are the relationships you consciously sought out different from those that came into your life as a matter of circumstance? Chances are, the relationships you desired and worked toward are generally of higher quality. Conversely, when we don't do our due diligence on the front end, relationships can struggle. Not to worry, though. You can transform the relationships you already have, and we'll give you a framework to cultivate relationships with intention and consciousness moving forward.

Your Relationships Shape Your Quality of Life

Relationships are imperatives in our lives. A 2011 study from Harvard Medical School found that "lack of strong relationships increased the risk of premature death from all causes by 50% — an effect on mortality risk roughly comparable to smoking up to 15 cigarettes a day, and greater than obesity and physical inactivity."[1] We cannot afford to ignore the quality of our relationships.

Relationships affect our mental health as well. A 2015 TED Talk by psychiatrist Robert Waldinger titled *What Makes a Good Life? Lessons from the Longest Study on Happiness* shared research that people in their eighties who had satisfying marriages had better mental health outcomes and that their moods didn't change even on days when they experienced more physical pain.[2]

Waldinger added, "Good relationships don't just protect our bodies; they protect our brains. And those good relationships, they don't have to be smooth all the time. Some of our octogenarian couples could bicker with each other day in and day out, but as long as they felt that they could really count on the other when the going got tough, those arguments didn't take a toll on their memories."[3]

---

1 Harvard Health Publishing. "Strengthen Relationships for Longer, Healthier Life - Harvard Health." *Harvard Health*, Harvard Health, 2019, www.health.harvard.edu/healthbeat/strengthen-relationships-for-longer-healthier-life.

2 Mineo, Liz. "Good Genes Are Nice, but Joy Is Better." *Harvard Gazette*, Harvard University, 11 Apr. 2017, news.harvard.edu/gazette/story/2017/04/over-nearly-80-years-harvard-study-has-been-showing-how-to-live-a-healthy-and-happy-life/.

3 Robert Waldinger. *What Makes a Good Life? Lessons from the Longest Study on Happiness | Robert Waldinger*. YouTube, 25 Jan. 2016, www.youtube.com/watch?v=8KkKuTCFvzI.

There is a direct correlation between the quality of our relationships and the quality of our lives. If you care about your happiness and you care about your health, then tending to the relationships in your life must be a priority.

Where's Your Focus?

We know we need healthy relationships in our lives, but how do we improve them if they already feel problematic or broken to us? Most people are focused on their relationships in a way that is causing them to feel strained. Remember the story of my ex-girlfriend and her constant attention to her insecurity? It's so easy to consciously and unconsciously focus on aspects of your relationship that cause a painful struggle. In doing so, however, you can lose sight of what is working and what you actually want.

In this book, we'll reframe your focus and create a new vision for the relationship you'd like to improve. Change starts with awareness—we cannot change what we cannot see. Once you pick a relationship to work on (we'll get to that soon), I invite you to explore how you are focusing on that relationship. Do you continue to focus on one or a few negative points? Are you thinking about everything you *don't* like or *don't* want in the relationship?

It becomes a lightbulb moment for people when they realize their relationships struggle because they are focused on everything that feels challenging. They focus on how their romantic partner isn't great at planning ahead and get frustrated when inevitable surprises arise. They focus on a colleague's lack of attention to detail and get annoyed every time they find an error. We take ourselves wherever we go, meaning how we show up in one relationship is often how we show up in other relationships. If we've been trained to focus on the issues rather than the outcome, we often end up with the same disastrous results.

Relationships can stay challenging or they can evolve. If we want things to improve, being open and willing to change how we view the relationship is an important piece. The great news is that when you change your focus dynamics in one relationship, it will uplevel all your relationships.

Imagine how life-changing that could be!

WHY ARE YOU READING THIS BOOK?

Each person may have a different reason for picking up this book. You may be looking for a deeper sense of connection with someone in your life. You may be looking to completely transform a relationship. You may be seeking a fulfilling and joyful relationship with a partner. Or perhaps you are looking at how to play the game better at work. If by chance you're only here because your partner hogtied you and they are forcing you to read this book…well, you're here now, so why not stop the struggle and see what you can get out of it?

Whatever your intention is, I'd like you to take a moment and imagine yourself at the end of this book. You've invested your time. You've gone through the exercises. You've had the conversations. You have done the work and are now getting the outcome you have always desired. What would that outcome be? Close your eyes and imagine it fully! Feel it in your essence! Claim it! Own it!

I have worked with thousands of clients on cultivating vibrant relationships through private and group sessions, classes, seminars, across social media, and on my podcast, *Joey's Performance Tune-Up*. The fascinating thing is that most people I work with are very accomplished and extraordinary individuals. They are people who are accustomed to succeeding. They are people who enjoy fulfillment in many aspects of their lives. They're highly competent in business, athletic, or creative pursuits. Yet, they struggle in relationships because they haven't had the opportunity to hone their skills when it comes to interacting with people in a healthy and productive way.

It's not a failure to be in this state. Recognizing you have one or more relationships in your life that you would like to change and improve is such an important first step. You want to do better and you're ready to show up and find out how. That is a sign of strength, not weakness.

Types of Relationships You Can Improve
Many of the principles discussed in this book apply to relationships with friends, romantic partners, family members, children, and colleagues. They can also apply to relationships with your boss or your customers. What seems to really surprise people is that the techniques in this book can also help you manage relationships with people who are deceased or that you're estranged from. Even if you can't have a two-way conversation with someone, it does not mean that you cannot evolve how you view and show up for that relationship.

The world goes round and round by how we manage our relationships. What people think of as emotional intelligence could be characterized as relationship intelligence. If it's not the single most imperative skill to have that will identify success and fulfillment in life, it's definitely in the top three. Regardless of the type of relationship, the rules, principles, and systems that make these relationships thrive are the same. That is great news in that what you learn and apply in one relationship can often be duplicated and applied to others.

Lastly, contrast is important to developing a well-rounded perspective and understanding of why we do what we do. So, in addition to learning the rules that help relationships work, we'll also address what makes relationships crumble. This book will guide you in avoiding these minefields and saboteurs.

I've had my own experiences of destroying many of my own relationships throughout the years. I have missed the mark, like any human being, over and over again. Whenever I miss a mark for myself, I have learned to get fascinated by it. It's why I've gotten into the world of personal development/human performance the way I have, and why I've gotten as good at it as I have.

You can too.

THE PARTS OF THIS BOOK

There are three aspects of every relationship, regardless of its nature. The first aspect of the relationship is you. The second aspect of the relationship is the relationship itself. The third aspect of the relationship is the other person. Understanding these three aspects simplifies understanding relationships. Not giving proper time and attention to each of the three aspects can complicate things.

Section 1: Ourselves

The first aspect of the relationship is you. How you show up in a relationship is impacted by the emotions you have, your thoughts, the things you say, and the things you do. The question to ask is, "Who do I need to be in the relationship to create the joy, happiness, cosmic love, or whatever else I'm looking to achieve in my relationships?"

In this section, we will focus heavily on your vision for life, and then your vision for the relationship you've chosen to work on. You'll learn my four steps for transformation, how to align yourself with your vision, and tools to build your emotional intelligence. Lastly, we'll dive into your imperatives for a relationship—what you truly need, and the things you want and desire.

Section Two: The Relationship

The second aspect of the relationship is the relationship itself. The relationship is the mixing of our ways of being with the other person's ways of being. This can be a beautiful creation or a complete disaster. And while no two relationships are exactly alike, because no two energies can come together and express outcomes in the exact same way, the tools for managing relationships are almost always the same.

In this section of the book, we'll dive into your expectations for the relationship and get clear on your needs, wants, and desires. Once you know your non-negotiables, you'll learn the tools for setting effective boundaries and how to communicate them with the other person. This section will also cover how relationships can be sabotaged (whether intentionally or unintentionally) and what is truly within your control in a relationship.

Section Three: The Other Person

The third aspect of a relationship is the other person. We can influence the other person, but we cannot control them. Each person enters the relationship with their own expectations. The other person has their own set of relationship needs for us to recognize and respond to.

While this section explores the relationship partially through the perspective of the other person, the reality is that we may be limited in our knowledge of where they're coming from. That is why this section is also focused once again on us, but this time through the lens of managing ourselves with the other person. It's about acknowledging how we *both* show up for the vision of the relationship and identifying who is responsible for what.

Pulling It All Together

I conclude the book with additional information and exercises to support you in taking action. It's about creating vibrant routines in your life so that you stay on the path toward the relationships and life you desire. I combine my years of diverse studies and experiences to share what I've found to be the most effective methods to continually promote positive growth and reinvention in my own life. Now it's your turn.

WHAT THIS BOOK WON'T DO

Over the years, I've had individuals and pairs walk through my door because they were at the breaking point of their relationship. Business partners were ready to dissolve the enterprise. One spouse had threatened the other with divorce. "Last-chance" opportunities had been given between family members. While we worked to improve the communication and understanding in their relationship, for some it was simply too late. Too many red flags had been ignored. Too much damage had been done.

If you're looking for a book to help you get clear on who was right and who was wrong in your troubled relationship, this is *not* the book for you. Having a narrow focus and assigning blame has never, in the history of all of my work and studies, brought about a positive relationship solution. The only way you "win" here is if you can get clear about the type of relationship you want to cultivate and are willing to lean in.

If you are absolutely willing to be authentic and transparent, take yourself apart a little bit, and then put yourself back together, you will finish this book as a different human being. You'll have access to a different possibility in relationships. No ifs, ands, or buts about it. You will have the set of skills and tools to continue to refine this process in any relationship you opt into.

Relationships are something you can never perfect. None of us are perfect in relationships. I'm not. It is something that we engage in over a lifetime and maybe we get to a level of mastery. There's always going to be new ways to grow. This book is an excellent starting point.

If there is one thing I wish I could communicate to the world it would be to not wait to work on the quality of your relationships. There are consequences to our inaction when we choose to let things slide because they're "not a big deal." Eventually, they will accumulate into a huge deal.

When you choose not to work on the quality of your relationships you are choosing one of two things—for them to be a struggle or for them to end. Most people would not choose either of those outcomes, and yet they still find themselves unwilling to take an honest look at their vision for life, their needs, wants, and desires in their relationships, and how they are showing up for that vision and those needs.

Do not be one of those people. Commit to learning how to become better in your relationships and it will serve you in all of them. Do not let the fear of being brutally honest with yourself and being vulnerable with others deter you from moving toward your most vibrant life. If you want to improve your life, you must improve your relationships. If you want to improve your relationships, you must be willing to do the work to change. Simply reading this book cannot make the changes for you.

YOUR TRAINING STARTS NOW

I'm going to make an invitation—read this book with a focus by choosing a specific relationship to tend to. If you simply read the book without a specific person in mind, you can still get a lot out of it, but you will not experience the same level of understanding and the same motivation to change. If you're serious about leveraging this book for growth, pick a specific relationship and you'll experience transformation.

Three ground rules that I ask you to adhere to with this book:

1. **Pick a specific person who is NOT yourself.** You will most certainly tend to yourself through the relationship that you pick, but you may not pick yourself. Also, don't use generalities. Don't write down "my friends," "my children," "my exes," or "my colleagues." Pick a specific individual that you have been in a relationship with, whether they're currently living or not. Read on for more about ways to pick a relationship.

2. **Be willing to transform this relationship.** You must be willing to have a different emotional experience regarding this person. It doesn't mean you have to interact with them. What this means is that you must be willing to stop doing something you are currently doing and start doing something that you have not done. (Notice how many times I said "you" there.)

3. Even if you're feeling a little fear, I invite you to **take action anyway.** You are in the driver's seat. You have to push the accelerator to make things move.

If you're debating which relationship you should choose to start with, I will tell you that there is generally no wrong answer. It all depends on what feels most energizing to you. Consider these three different ways to approach who you pick:

1. You can pick the specific relationship where you experience the **greatest challenge**. Maybe it's a relationship with a child. Perhaps you think of an ex—maybe it's been several years, and you'd like to let go of the anger and animosity tied to that person. Maybe you think of a parent, even if they are no longer alive or you're estranged from them. Imagine how life-changing it would feel to improve upon your greatest relationship challenge!

2. You can pick the person who is **most important** to you. Pick a relationship you care about most and consider how you would like to optimize it. If you look at your life, who is the

person that you wish you had a better relationship with? It doesn't have to be that your current relationship is bad or challenging, but you know there's room for improvement. If the person is really important to you and you don't want the relationship to slide further apart, choose to work on that relationship and move it into a healthier place.

3. You can choose the relationship where there's the **greatest opportunity**. What I mean by opportunity is it's somebody you interact with a lot. It's a relationship that, if evolved, could create a greater sense of happiness and fulfillment within yourself. What is a relationship that has the potential to make many wonderful things possible in your world? Is it your boss who is in charge of your next promotion? Is it your child whom you find to be in a regular state of frustration or anxiety? Perhaps it's a coworker with whom you have to collaborate regularly. Improve the relationship that will help you grow.

It's time to grab a notebook, open a Google Doc, or take a voice note on your phone and complete both exercises before moving on to the next chapter.

EXERCISE 1:
Name the thing you would like to get out of this book.

Maybe it's an outcome you'd like to create. Maybe it's a change you desire. Maybe it's something you want to draw into your life. Take a moment and write it down as your intention.

Now, imagine you're at the end of this book. Imagine once again what has occurred for you. Maybe it has to do with your spouse. Or perhaps there's a dynamic you'd like to evolve with your children. Simply write down your intention and desired outcome for reading this book.

EXERCISE 2:
Write the top three things you'd like to learn or know about yourself and relationships, by the time you complete this book.

If you could ask for any wisdom as it pertains to relationships, what would be the top three things you'd like to understand? What skills would you like to learn, access, or develop as it relates to relationships? How could they help you in other areas of your life?

PART 1
OURSELVES

CHAPTER 1
IT STARTS WITH A VISION

IN ORDER TO CREATE WHAT YOU WANT,
YOU HAVE TO NAME WHAT YOU WANT.

If you had asked me as a teenager what I was going to be when I grew up, my answer wouldn't have come anywhere close to what I'm doing right now. I don't mean that I don't absolutely love what I'm doing and the life I've created—I do! But as a teen, I couldn't have imagined that the life I lead today was even a possibility. For a long time, I was without a vision. I had no plan, no direction, and no idea where to even start. This is how people end up going through the motions of life instead of living.

My vision came when I took the time to get clear on what I wanted and needed out of life. Yes, this vision evolved over time, and no, I do not get upset with my clients if their visions evolve too. They should—we're human. But you must have a starting point to know where you're going. Before we can dive into what you want out of your relationships, you need to get clear on what you want out of life.

We are going to start this vibrant relationship journey by taking a holistic look at life. This is the groundwork that is required in order to understand how each relationship supports your overall vision for life…or doesn't. Do not skip forward. Do not tell yourself that you'll get to visioning later.

This is the most important chapter you will read in this book because everything from here forward is going to point back to vision. It is the gas for your car. Without it, you'll just be sitting there wondering why things aren't moving for you. Got it? Great!

VISION OBSTACLES

Your mind may already be generating obstacles to this vision exercise. The most common struggle I see is when someone has a relationship in their life, usually with a romantic partner or a business partner, in which the other person does not seem aligned with the vision. I hear things like, "What do I do if my person doesn't really fit with what I want…but we have three kids and a whole life together?" Or, "What if my business partner and I are at odds over key issues in our business but we're legally bound?"

The answer is, don't panic. Do your best to tune into yourself first. What do *you* want for yourself in these key areas of life? We do our relationship work from the inside out, which means we start with you. Remember, the relationships in your life are there to support your vision for life. Not the other way around.

A HOLISTIC VIEW OF LIFE

To start creating the vision for our lives, it's important to examine five key areas: health, career, family, lifestyle, and intimacy. How much do you know about yourself and what you desire in each of these areas? How close or far are you from your ideal vision? Let's take some time to explore what each of these key areas means.

Body & Health

What do you want around the body and health for yourself? What do you value? Are you at the gym every day? Do you prioritize organic, free-range, and grass-fed foods? Are you an aspiring biohacker, always looking to optimize your metabolism and gut biome? Maybe you're a foodie who loves exotic ingredients and indulgent dishes, aspiring to hit all the Michelin-star restaurants in the Western Hemisphere, dairy intolerance be damned!

Perhaps you're in chronic pain and working out is the last thing on your mind. Your vision of optimal body health might be a reduction in symptoms or an increase in basic mobility. Maybe you've struggled with mental health challenges or traumas in your life that you would like to be free from. What's your *thing* around body and health?

Career & Wealth

What do you want for yourself when it comes to your career? Some may desire to be a successful, international business mogul, pouring every waking hour into your business to become a household name. Others dream of Tim Ferriss's concept of the four-hour workweek. Do you want to work for someone else and "turn off" work at the end of each day? Do you crave the excitement and novelty of entrepreneurship and always solving for new ways of doing things?

What do you aspire to when it comes to wealth? Does wealth mean being a multimillionaire or being able to retire before fifty? Are you a family-focused person who wants to have your needs met, maybe a little more, and prioritize adventures and experiences? Are you a spender or a saver? What's important to you about career and wealth?

Family, Kids, & Community

Think about the relationships you desire in your life. What does family mean to you, and what would your ideal family situation be? Are you in a partnership or married? Are you close to your family of origin or seeking instead to find your "chosen family" who understands and accepts you?

Are children part of the picture? If so, how many? Are they your children biologically, by way of adoption, or some other path? Are you in a partnership raising those children or opting for single parenthood? What's important to you around children and family?

What types of relationships do you desire with your coworkers, with friends, or within your community? Do you crave a large and diverse friend group or a few deep friendships? Do you want coworkers who challenge you and push you to be better, or do you have other visions of whom you work with and how? What types of relationships do you desire in your life?

Lifestyle & Experiences

This is one of the most fun categories and sometimes the greatest challenge for my clients. What's your idea of a good time? How do you have fun? What do you want to experience in your life that has meaning, feels fulfilling, or is important to you?

Think about day-to-day lifestyle, but also "bucket list" experiences. Are you a cozy-up-on-the-couch-and-watch-your-favorite-show type of person? Are you always on the go and don't feel complete unless you've hiked, biked, or skied on the daily? When you travel, is it rustic camping or are you staying at the Ritz? What's important to you about your lifestyle and experiences?

Intimacy & Sex

This area of life is one where our vision and desire may change over time due to our biology, health, and life circumstances. At this time in your life, what does intimacy mean for you in both the physical and emotional sense? When do you feel most intimately connected with another person? How often do you desire that?

What do you want for yourself around sex? More adventure? Consistency and safety? Do you share everything and have a vibrant, passionate sexual relationship, or does sex no longer hold importance in your life? What do you want for your life in terms of intimacy and sex?

PULLING IT ALL TOGETHER

Having context for what we want for ourselves and for our lives allows us to transform and design relationships to support that vision. The relationships you have in your life are not neutral—they're either moving you toward or taking you away from your vision for life.

This work is so important that I have an entire curriculum that explores in greater depth how to name vision, create benchmarks, and develop an action plan to fulfill vision: Power of Vision. Learn more about it in the Resources section of this book.

Once you have your vision for life, you can invite the people in your life to show up in a way that supports the manifestation of your vision.

EXERCISE: Creating Your Life Vision

1. Grab a notebook or your computer and write down each of the five key areas we just discussed. Allow your mind and heart to explore what you desire in each of those areas. Write it down! It's important for you to write openly and freely so you'll have something to refer back to when you find yourself falling into old patterns. Name your vision for your life!

2. Be willing to believe it's possible. You've got to make it important so you take action toward it. Sit with what you wrote and envision it daily. See it as if it's already happened in your life and you are living it now.

3. Acknowledge it daily. Measure and evaluate consistently to align your actions with it.

If you are willing to do these three things, you can have the things you want in any relationship.

YOUR VISION FOR YOUR RELATIONSHIP

Once we have a vision for what we want out of life, it helps us to more clearly identify what we want out of our relationships. Again, for the sake of this book, we are not going to focus on all your relationships, just the one you chose in the first section of this book. Know that there is no right or wrong here. Simply tune in to yourself and name what's important for you to know inside of this relationship.

Twenty years ago, before I did all this work with people, I thought I had a very clear idea of what was right or wrong in a relationship. I had many strongly held ideas about the way things were supposed to be. I've since learned that any time we assume something is "supposed to be" a certain way, we're setting ourselves up for resentment, disappointment, and failure.

Over time and through working with more people, I perpetually had my mind blown by what people enjoyed and wanted to create and experience in their relationships. I realized through working with people that *my* definition of "right" and "wrong" in relationships was far too narrow and naive. We don't all want the same things—not in love, not in business partnerships, not with our family members.

Seeking "Normal" Relationships

I invite you to be honest and transparent with yourself as you engage the questions posed to you throughout this book. Like I had to do, I invite you to explore what it feels like to suspend your notions of right or wrong to see what *really* matters to you in your relationship.

Do you know what working with thousands of people from all over the world on their relationship struggles has taught me? Normal is only a setting on your dryer. There is no such thing as a normal relationship. This may be hard to believe at first because we often look at other relationships from an outsider's perspective and think, "Wow, *that's* a great relationship between that parent and their child!" or "What a perfect couple!" You may think back to your own parents and aspire to have a marriage that seems as solid and stable as theirs appeared to you. Our metric for how we judge a "good" relationship is often based not on any of the relationships we're in but on the relationships we've observed.

The problem is, in most other relationships you are often not privy to their inner workings. What you see is a momentary interaction between two individuals that allows you to create a whole fantasy about how it is for them. I would bet that if you tried living or working with them for one week, your perspective might shift. I'm not saying this to be negative or to insinuate that they *don't* actually have a good relationship, but it's important for you to recognize that there is no one-size-fits-all perfect approach to human interaction. What works for one relationship cannot work identically for you and another person. No two people do it the same. When you attach yourself to a notion of a perfect or normal relationship, you can't get where you need to go to achieve what you really want.

Now there is one thing that I have observed consistently from working with people and their relationships—they want to be happy. People want to feel connection and fulfillment. How each person accesses connection and fulfillment and how they get these needs met is unique to each individual. While one person might desire a relationship full of adventurous travel to feel fulfilled, another person might get a similar sense of fulfillment from deep conversation. Fulfillment may also look like the amount of time you and the other person spend with each other. What makes you feel a sense of happiness, connectedness, and fulfillment is yours to determine.

I would say that those are the core experiences people want to create and know in their relationships, regardless of the dynamics or the variations that show up. From those core desires, what we seek grows and expands from there. So shake off the idea of "normal," otherwise you're creating rules of engagement that are keeping you from what you really want.

CREATING YOUR RELATIONSHIP VISION

When it comes to creating a vision for what we want for our relationship, we are going to focus on three important areas: Being, Doing, and Having. You may be creating this vision for your relationship with your significant other, your parent, or your coworker. You can even create this vision for a relationship that you don't yet have but that you desire, like a new business partner or a romantic partner.

There is an important piece I need you to keep in mind as you create this vision for your relationship. You must create your vision for the relationship as if you weren't already in the current relationship. What that means is that you're pretending like you get to wipe the slate clean. Envision your relationship with the other person as if you're starting over and building it from scratch.

Do not allow what you know about them or the challenges of your current situation to influence your vision for the relationship. This is not the time to put limitations on what you desire or let any bias you may hold influence what you want your relationship to look like. It is crucial that you do not define your vision for the relationship based on what you don't want or what you perceive as going wrong.

Establishing Clear Lines

It's important when you list what you want in each category of Being, Doing, and Having that you make sure you're not blurring the categories. *Being* relates to your inner state and how you feel—adjectives like "joyful" and "energized." *Doing* are the actions and activities you want—verbs like "running" or "resting." *Having* refers to the things and stuff that you want in your life—nouns like "cabin" or "labradoodle."

The reason we need to be so crystal clear in our differentiation is that the three categories are not dependent on each other, though many people assume that they are. Take for example my client, Bryan. Bryan is very well-off financially. He's been married to his college sweetheart for many years, and they have two healthy teenage children. Bryan wants to feel happiness and contentment in his family relationships. He also loves boating and going on luxurious vacations. For many years, Bryan assumed that his wealth and ability to take his family on extravagant vacations would create his desired feelings of happiness. They didn't at all. His entire family was miserable for their most recent yacht excursion.

You can't create your desired Being just by Having or Doing. And what you desire to Do doesn't always guarantee that it will get you what you want to Have. As we move into the next exercise, approach each category as the unique vision that it is. You'll find that when you start living from a place of alignment with your vision, you can often achieve what you desire in each of the categories.

Being

Being is your inner experience of reality. When naming any vision, we start with emotion first. What emotional experiences would you like to enjoy in the relationship? What way of Being do you want to experience and bring to the relationship? I have never known someone to proclaim that they would like to know more stress, more anger, more insecurity. They are typically seeking things like love, joy, and inspiration. Keep in mind that not everyone will name or value emotions the same. Joy may mean and matter more to you, while another person may value passion and inspiration. What emotional experiences are you seeking to know in your relationship?

Doing

Next, we need to name what we want to be Doing in this relationship. Doing is what we're up to in life. Are we building a business together? Are we off on athletic adventures? Are we going on walking tours of European cities? Are we having the extended family over for Sunday dinner? Are we taking turns planning an epic annual friends trip? Are we curled up on the couch watching our favorite cooking shows? Our Doing are the actions we are taking in our lives.

If you're finding yourself writing things you're currently Doing, go back and revisit your vision for life. Is your vision aligned with how you spend your hours each day? If your current Doing doesn't fit your life vision, what is it that you want to be Doing in life and this relationship?

Having

Finally, we can name our desires for things—the Having. Having is specific stuff, or the logistics of what is necessary for our Doing. For example, if your Doing involves going on a spa trip with friends, your Having would be things like the type of spa you're going to, the specific hotel you want to stay at, the airline class you want to fly for this trip, and the funds to make it happen. If the relationship you're focused on is a business partnership, name what you want to Have in the business—revenue, number of employees, number of clients, and impact marks. For a romantic relationship, your Having might be thinking ahead to a family with two children, a big dog, and a house on a lake. Having is the "things and stuff" that allow us to do the things we want to do.

EXERCISE: Creating Your Relationship Vision

Grab your computer and notepad and write the Being, Doing, and Having of the relationship that you've chosen to explore through this book. Check back with your vision for life to make sure that the things you've listed in each category align with it.

RELATIONSHIP CHALLENGES

One of my favorite Doings in my adult life is driving Porsche cars on a track. What can I say, I have a love for speed! But the Porsche racing centers don't just hand you the keys and say, "Good luck, buddy!" In the initial learning period, an instructor drove while I sat by as passenger to observe and learn. That was my role at that time, and I was responsible for fulfilling the expectation that was set.

Eventually, I got behind the wheel and the instructor sat in the passenger seat. It was my time to take what I had learned and apply it. The instructor offered guidance as I went. We were both fulfilling our roles based on the boundaries and expectations of the program. If at any point I had leaned over from the passenger seat and took control of the wheel from the instructor as he was driving, or if he left his passenger seat to try and control the wheel while I had my feet on the gas, we would be violating the expectations set and setting ourselves up for some serious danger!

Why do I share this? Because it's a loose metaphor for how relationships work. We're here on this journey around the course together, but each person has their role and what they're responsible for. Many times in relationships I see people don't want to focus on what they're doing but instead want to control what the other person is doing. If I leaned over from the passenger side and tried to take control of another driver's wheel, we'd be in serious trouble. (Not to mention, they'd probably be infuriated with me). I would be equally mad if I were driving and they tried to control the car for me. I most definitely would not be invited back to the Porsche track.

Control in Relationships

It doesn't feel good to control other people, and it doesn't feel good to be controlled. At the same time, I commonly see people in relationships who think that the only way to achieve their vision is to control what the other person is doing or how they're behaving. It's a huge mistake and one that will leave you both exhausted and frustrated. I will say it over and over in this book: the only person you can control is yourself.

Start by checking in with yourself. Where are you emotionally right now? Where are you emotionally in your relationship? Now own those feelings as your own, completely. What I mean by that is to realize that what you are feeling is completely on you. It's *your* nervous system and *your* emotions. You are the only person who can manage those things.

The other person did not "make you" feel sad or disappointed. They did not "make you" yell or cry. You might be thinking to yourself, "What are you talking about, Joey? Of course, they did!" I get it. We're often raised to believe that our actions and words create the emotional states of another. We have been raised with the stories that if a person does *this*, then we should feel *that*.

The person may have done something that warrants you feeling sad, angry, or diminished. It doesn't mean that you *have to* have any of those emotional responses though. Think about it this way: If they act poorly and you respond with an emotional energy that you do not want to hold, your emotion doesn't necessarily do anything for the other person. What your emotional energy does is define the experience for yourself. And the reality is that when someone mistreats you, you don't deserve to feel in an unaligned emotional state. You deserve to feel better!

Let's illustrate that. My client, Savannah, came to me because she was at her wit's end with how she and her husband argued. His tone often left her feeling like she was being yelled at. It would send her nervous system into fight or flight and she would move into the emotional energy of fear, sadness, and isolation. She would shut down, and they could never seem to have a two-way conversation to work through their conflicts.

Savannah and I did a lot of work to identify the emotional energies she desires to be in, those of love and compassion, even in the face of someone who was not showing up well. We worked through her taking control of her nervous system with the Four-Sided Breath exercise and other tools that you'll learn later in this chapter. Once she felt she had control over her nervous system and had a clear vision of the emotional energy she desired to be in, she began to show up differently when her husband raised his voice. And because she chose a different energy, it influenced the way her husband responded. He lowered his volume and began to choose his words differently.

When someone shows up in a contracted energy, like fear or anger, we often respond in the same contracted way. When we can show up with expansive energy, in a higher state of being, we have the ability to positively influence those around us. This becomes an eye-opening revelation for people when they take back control of their emotional state instead of blaming it on the other person. It is freeing to know that they are not responsible for your emotional pattern, just as you are not responsible for theirs. Once you experience that, your consciousness evolves and you start entering spaces and situations from a new, expansive perspective.

One of my hopes for you with this book is that you feel great within yourself. If you're in an expansive space as you-with-you, then you'll have greater clarity of the vision of life you want to experience, the things you want, and things you don't want. You'll realize that your vision is going to match up with some people and not with others.

From this point forward, do not attempt to make yourself feel better by controlling what other people do. That's where relationships break down. Understand that learning to control your nervous system and emotional state are not skills you can acquire quickly or simply because you desire them. They take repeated training and development.

There are people and relationships in which behavior truly is unhealthy, unsafe, or unaligned with your vision for life. Later in this book, we are going to discuss boundaries, healthy and unhealthy dynamics, and expectations so that you can assess and manage your relationships more effectively. Understand, though, that you can never make your happiness dependent on the actions of another person. That's like giving someone else the steering wheel of your car and hoping they take you in the right direction. Realize that you control your own nervous system. You have to be in control of how you feel and where you're headed. They are the passenger for you, accompanying you on your journey!

Remember My Ex-Girlfriend?

Do you remember the story I shared in the intro of this book about my ex-girlfriend with insecurity issues? That relationship is a perfect example of what happens when another person tries to make us responsible for how they feel, or where we think that our actions can manipulate their responses.

If I think about it today, I would never be in a situation with a person like that now because I would choose not to opt in with them in the first place. Her initial request of asking me to use my actions and behaviors to change her feelings would be a huge red flag to me today. What I wish I had known back then was that she was probably in the remnants of trauma due to past relationships and circumstances in her life. She was acting out past patterns in the present day. This is why even when someone is focused on you in a certain way that may feel derogatory or hurtful, it's important to understand that it's often not about you and is not something you need to take personally.

If I had acknowledged that, then I would have realized that her requests, actions, and behaviors had nothing to do with me. I would have gone to her and let her know that I cared about her and that she was important to me. I would remind her that she didn't need to run and would be safe. With the knowledge I have today, my conversations with her would have been very different.

I hope that is somewhat reassuring to you that if you are in a relationship that feels problematic, there are ways that you can take action and communicate differently to set better expectations and boundaries. You do not have to throw in the towel on a relationship just because the other person has unresolved and unconscious internal patterns. We all get a bit crazy when our emotional patterns get activated. We all act in peculiar ways when it comes to past wounds.

Repeating Patterns

When my ex-girlfriend left for the airport, I vividly remember sitting down on the couch and asking myself, "Why is it that all women are crazy?" And then I realized something important—they're not, I was just picking the ones who showed up in the same erratic, demanding, and unpredictable ways.

Through the gift of hindsight, I realized that I had been in the same relationship dynamics with several women. Have you found that too? Are there repeating patterns in the way that people in your life show up? Throughout this section of the book, we'll explore why you may be consistently opting in for these dynamics. You'll gain insight into how you're showing up on your end of the relationship, what you're putting into it, and why you're getting similar outcomes with different people. Once you can recognize your unconscious patterns and retrain those patterns to align with your vision, your relationships after that will be unrecognizable from before. If you're ready to get serious about owning this process and your patterns, you can engage in our Power Series training. You can find more information in the Resources section of this book, or visit innermatrixsystems.com.

FIVE STEPS TO TRANSFORM YOUR LIFE

It's not enough to have a vision. We need to train a more intentional way of being with ourselves and in our relationships. That is the process of transformation.

Learning and practicing the art of inner training and evolving your inner matrix gives you the skills that you can apply not only to your relationships but to any aspect of your life to drive you toward your vision. In all of my studies and practices, with teachers from around the globe, I have learned that there are five main principles of inner training. Reading them is easy. The real test is in the doing.

It may be a challenge, but I can assure you that if you're willing to do the work it will be worth it. The principles taught in this book, the methods that you're going to lean into, have the ability to completely redefine your experience of any relationship. They have the power to completely transform any relationship currently in your life.

Five Steps to Transformation:

1. **Understand**: Learn the "why" behind a specific tool, technique, or strategy before executing. Doing so will help you commit to taking action.

2. **Experience**: Once you understand, you must execute the technique or strategy to experience what it's like to do it. If you don't have the experience of execution, then the tool, technique, or strategy stays in the understanding phase, which will never produce an outcome.

3. **Confirm**: This is one of the most important steps—you can execute a technique a thousand times, but if you are executing improperly you will not get the result. So often people don't get a result and they blame the training, when in fact it's improper execution that's keeping the result from them.

4. **Repeat**: Training is repetition. Mastery is training. Train and repeat proper execution until it becomes a natural reflex.

5. **Realize**: Realization is the step where the tool and technique become part of who you are. You no longer have to think about executing; it happens without conscious thought. You have the outcome and are living it.

Easy, right? But what does this look like in real life? Let's use the simple example of my work in martial arts.

The first step, understanding, meant more than just knowing the basics of how to move. I had to understand the history behind this art and combat form I was studying. I had to learn the physical, mental, and energetic components. I had to understand the intention (the "why") behind each movement and when and how to use it. Now think about it in terms of your relationship. What are all of the areas of your relationship that you would like to try and understand? What skills do you think you'll need? And let's not forget the most important question—what is your vision and driving force behind this transformation? What is your "why"?

Secondly, we have to experience a skill or technique. Reading, listening, or taking a class are a great starting point, but they are not enough. Real-life application is where you learn nuance and why some things work at certain times, while other situations require a different approach. What do you think you'll need to experience in your relationship for it to transform?

The next steps, Confirm and Repeat, are two of the most important. It's not enough for us to simply experience the technique; we need to execute it correctly, over and over again. The old saying "practice makes perfect" is incorrect. If you practice something wrong, even if you do it for 10,000 hours, you'll just be really good at doing it incorrectly. We need to strive for as close to perfect practice as possible if we want to master something. It reminds me of the Bruce Lee quote, "I fear not the man who has practiced 10,000 kicks once, but I fear the man who has practiced one kick 10,000 times."

This means having a solid understanding, doing the work to prepare, and executing the same correct skill over and over again until it becomes ingrained in our minds or muscle memory. This is how we create reflexes. This is when we know we've transformed. Our new way of being has become a part of us. The skills that we learn and apply in one relationship will work and apply in all relationships because we have changed ourselves. That is how we know we've reached the final step in transformation—realization.

CHAPTER 2
YOUR ALIGNMENT WITH VISION

*YOU'RE EITHER MOVING TOWARD VISION
OR YOU'RE HEADED SOMEWHERE ELSE.*

I've mentioned it already, but it's worth repeating: we take ourselves wherever we go. In my book *The Inner Matrix*, I cover inner pattern dynamics that we carry within and then live those patterns out in our lives. The more work you do on yourself and the greater your awareness of your own patterning, the better the result you'll have in your relationships. It all goes back to you, which is why it is so important that you stay in alignment and focused on your vision.

You might be thinking, "But Joey, that's ridiculous! If I know what my vision is, then why would I take any action that *wouldn't* lead me toward that vision?" Because current unconscious pattern dynamics don't align with that vision and need to be retrained to access a different reality. That is the reason why vision requires transformation. Transformation takes work. Sometimes that work is stuff people don't want to admit or address. We have tendencies like self-doubt, procrastination, and other means of self-sabotage that we allow to steer us off course. My hope is that your desire for a vibrant life is greater than any inner patterning that might try to convince you to fail. You deserve better!

WHAT YOU PUT INTO YOUR RELATIONSHIPS

There are four things people put into a relationship, even if they're not in the same room together. Both you and your person, right now at this moment, are putting these four things into your relationship. You are influencing each other and you are impacting each other through these things right now.

"What?" you might ask. "I thought the last chapter said we are not responsible for managing another person's emotions." You are correct, and I'm glad you're paying attention. It's an important distinction. One person's actions do not directly cause the other person's emotions or reactions. However, how you show up will certainly (though out of your control) impact the other person and may influence how they show up.

Here are the things we are both putting into a relationship:

Emotions

The first thing we put into a relationship is our emotional energy. When you show up in different emotional energies, you are sensed and received differently. The same goes for the emotional energy of others. Think about it. When you've been around someone in the energy of anger, how did your own energy feel? What about when you've been in the company of someone who has the energy of joy? We are more intimately connected to the people in our lives than we may even realize.

When I was twenty and working my glamorous job selling electronics at Circuit City, I was suddenly struck with the feeling that my good friend Alex was not okay. Something was wrong, though I didn't know what or why. I just felt it like a sudden pang that hit me. It was an eerie feeling. When I called Alex, it immediately went to his voicemail recording, which was now a melancholy song with some worrisome lyrics. My boss was kind enough to let me take off for the day, and I raced over to Alex's home where I found a suicide note on his table. I called a few of our closest friends to come over to his house.

Shortly thereafter, Alex's car pulled into his driveway. He had just driven to a cliff and was planning to take his own life when he was struck with the feeling that he had to go home and that he could finish his plan another day. When he saw us there, he burst into tears. He thought nobody cared, and he felt alone. Fortunately, we all listened to our inner knowing and felt the emotional pull that ultimately saved his life.

That was my first exposure to realizing how connected we are to those in our lives. People could have explained to me that we have energetic connections and, to some degree, I could have intellectualized it to get my brain on board that it was probably real. Experiencing it firsthand gave me a whole new level of understanding. Have you ever experienced something similar?

We are connected to people. The closer we are, the more connected we are and the more impact we have. This connection spans time and space. It is our emotional energy that goes into the relationship. How important is it to manage our emotional energy? I have an entire curriculum on mastering your emotional self, called Power of Emotion, to support people who struggle to show up in the emotional energy that is aligned with moving them toward their relationship and life's vision. In the Power of Emotion intensive (described in the Resources section of this book), we train you to manage and master your emotional energy through three key steps:

1. Become aware of and sensitive to emotions that are occurring.

2. Learn to center and turn the emotions off.

3. Activate and access new emotions that will support you and align with your vision.

Thoughts & Beliefs

The second thing we put into our relationships are our thoughts and beliefs. Our thoughts and beliefs may or may not be true (or true for others), but they are stories and systems that we hold with some level of importance. Some thoughts are fleeting, but those that recur with frequency often inform our belief system. What we believe in most strongly is often tied to our values, those tenets we hold most sacred or important in our lives. Because we are exposed to different people and life experiences that create our thoughts, it is easy to see how our beliefs are different from others' and why we can grow up to value different things. For a deeper dive into thoughts and beliefs, refer to my Power of Focus curriculum. More information can be found in the Resources section of this book.

Our Words

Words, what we say and how we say it, hold power. In Don Miguel Ruiz's book *The Four Agreements*, the first and arguably most important agreement is to "be impeccable with your word." It's the recognition that the language we choose to use is critical to how we show up. If our words come from a place of fear, they will impact the receiver far differently than if they came from a place of love. How we use our words is a technique that takes repeated great practice to master. Communication is an art, and our thoughts become our words. It's a skill set that is worth training to master.

Our Actions

The fourth thing we put into our relationships is our actions, the things we do. I'm sure you've had relationships with people who are all words and no action. Think about the impact that has had on you and your relationship with that person. Our actions, or lack thereof, are often very much within our control and can have a tremendous impact on the quality of our relationships. But we have to own up to them.

We bring these four things to every relationship, and the other person brings all four of them too. We can control our emotions, thoughts, words, and actions, but we can't control the other person's. Think through what that means. That means we have to drop the expectation that somehow we can get them to say the exact words we want them to say or do exactly what we want them to do. They need to show up for that.

If you want a better relationship—I cannot recommend this enough—go first! Take ownership of your own emotions, thoughts, words, and actions. Show up in a way that will influence the relationship to thrive, because you can and because you deserve it.

DON'T MANAGE THE PERSON, MANAGE THE VISION

Now that we know our responsibility is not to attempt to manage the other person, we can be laser-focused on what we are responsible for: managing our vision. We manage our vision by looking at the four things we put into the relationship. Use those four areas as though you already have the aligned relationship you envision. From this perspective, you can ask yourself, "Am I showing up in a way that aligns with this vision or not?"

Our emotional state is an important piece in how we show up and influence the relationship we're in. Therefore, you must develop the skills, until they become reflexes, to identify the emotional state you are in and the capacity to align your emotions with your vision at any given time.

Follow these four steps to assess your emotional state:

1. **Name it.** Name your current emotional state. Is it love-based or fear-based? From a neurological perspective, fear-based emotions (such as sadness and anxiety) activate our fight-or-flight response and leave us feeling energetically contracted. Conversely, love-based emotional states (such as compassion, peace, and serenity) come from our prefrontal cortex and feel energetically expansive. Learn to give a name to the thoughts and feelings that are occurring to you. Check in with yourself and ask, "What am I feeling and what am I thinking?" If you

cannot name the specific emotion yet, see if you can identify whether it is love-based or fear-based.

2. **Evaluate it.** Ask yourself if your emotions and thoughts are aligned with the vision of what you want to create and experience in your relationship. If they are not aligned, pause before initiating any conversation with the other person. Do not take action until you are aligned.

3. **Align it.** Recognize that you are 100 percent responsible for your thoughts and your emotions. If you are out of alignment with your vision, you must realign to the thoughts and emotions that move you toward your vision.

4. **Take action.** Once you can confirm that you're in an aligned state, you're going to take action from that state.

You can start practicing this immediately. Right before your next conversation with someone, go through the four steps to assess where you're at from an emotional state. Determine if that is the emotional state you want to be in (the one that aligns with your vision or takes you away from it). For example, compassion moves you *toward* your vision, while resentment would move you *away* from it. The better you get at these four steps, the more your relationships will improve. Eventually, you'll master your end of a relationship, regardless of its nature.

One final note here: the following exercise does not work if you're not being honest with yourself. Don't name the emotion you *want* to feel and then pat yourself on the back. Just naming it doesn't create alignment. If you are feeling agitated, hurt, or sad, own it! Acknowledge it! You do yourself no favors by trying to convince yourself that you are feeling something you aren't. The point of this book is not to make you a better actor, it's to make you a better person. If you really want to train your emotional capacity at a deeper level and get clear on these essential fundamentals, check out my book *The Inner Matrix* and our Power Series Intensives. For more information on these, see the Resources section of this book.

ALIGNMENT CHECK

How important is it to be aligned as we move toward our vision? While I will spare you another car metaphor and what happens when our alignment is off, I can't help but think of the stories I've heard of the change in destination that would occur if an airplane altered its flight course by just 1 percent. Depending on the distance traveled, one could find themselves in a wildly different place than anticipated.

We can think about this in the positive in that shifting ourselves to an aligned state before we proceed, even if the change feels slight, gives us a far better chance of reaching our destination, our vision. Conversely, if we allow ourselves to operate when we're out of alignment, it's nearly impossible to get to where we desire to go.

Think about the vision you hold for the relationship you're tending. Ask yourself honestly and authentically, "Am I aligned with my vision in this relationship?" There's a high likelihood that you're not. That's okay. That is something you can change, and I'm glad you're here to do the work.

Take a moment to own any misalignment you may have. Allow yourself to connect to a healthy bit of guilt or shame for a moment.

But (and it's a big "but") be mindful not to disempower yourself in the process. Guilt and shame are valid emotions, but don't obsess over the fact that something is wrong or off. Negative self-talk only serves to diminish yourself. Focusing on the notion of failure or perceiving yourself as broken will not serve you to align with your vision.

Instead, I invite you to engage in any or all of these empowering statements to relate to yourself:

- I'm learning and growing
- I'm worthy and capable
- I acknowledge what's going well
- I'm on my way to my vision

Repeat these affirmative statements to yourself when you find that you're in a loop of negative self-talk and allow them to shift you back into aligned action. Write them. Speak them out loud. Repeat them until you are feeling in a better state about the work you are doing.

Own Your State

If you want the relationship and life you envision, you must take ownership of your state of being first. You have to know where you are starting from. If we are in a fear-based emotion and we can honestly acknowledge that, then we can also take the necessary steps to get out of that state. The way to get out of the emotion is simple… but not always easy.

The first step is to **name it**. You can't change something you cannot see or name. Naming your emotion may be as simple as "I feel sad" or "I feel angry." You don't necessarily have to understand the deep inner workings of why you feel that way, you just need to be honest about what you're feeling.

The second step can be a tricky one. It's imperative that you **own it**. "I feel sad because I feel sad. It's because of me." Your emotions are not because of what's happening. They are not because of what the other person is doing. It's not because the other person won't listen to you. It's not because they cheated on you. It's not because they pay more attention to the dog than you. Own it. "I feel sad. This is *my* sadness."

That may sound harsh at first, but it is actually an empowering action. When you put blame or responsibility on another person for the way that you are feeling, you give away your power to circumstances you cannot control or change. When you take full ownership of your emotions, you take full ownership of the power to change them. You are in control of your life. That is an excellent place to be.

Client Case Study: Owning Your State

Samantha joined my program and was hoping to create a vibrant relationship with Jeff, her husband of many years. Samantha shared with me that her current state of feeling toward Jeff was disgust. A healthy, active lifestyle had been important early on in their relationship, but Jeff stopped taking care of himself years ago. He was eating garbage like a teenager and rarely moved away from the TV. Samantha shared, "This kind of neglect has long-term consequences to our lives. I am not signing up to take care of someone who gets sick constantly because he failed to take care of himself. And honestly, it's just not sexy. This is *not* the man I married, and I'm afraid he's setting a terrible example for our daughters!"

I said to her, "What Jeff is doing is okay." Those were not the words she was hoping to hear. Now, slightly more agitated, Samantha asked, "What's the difference between okay and agreeing with his behavior?" *This* is the challenge of acceptance.

I replied that Jeff's actions were absolutely okay for him to do, for himself. Whatever he was doing was okay for him to do, for him. I pointed out to her that wanting to force him to change those behaviors was keeping her stuck, because those behaviors were out of her control. So long as she continued to try to control him, she was going to suffer. She was trying to force him to do something different than what he was choosing for himself.

This is where ownership begins. Samantha had to be willing to accept that it was okay for him to do what he was doing, as an action for him. She was ignoring the fact that she, too, had a choice in this relationship and this behavior all along. This was her time to decide if that behavior was okay for her and if it aligned with her vision of the relationship she wanted. Was her emotional energy going to take her to where she wanted?

I continued, "If Jeff's behavior has been okay with you for a very long time, then no longer blame him. Own it for yourself. You have accepted that this is okay for you. You've been willing to opt into this behavior for a number of years. That's okay."

This is where we start to discover that our choices in our emotional state dictate whether we are moving toward our vision or away from it. From this point forward, Samantha could choose to opt into the pattern of disgust and see what resulted. (Spoiler alert: it would not change Jeff's behavior). Or she could choose a new emotional pattern dynamic that would move her closer to her vision.

We started by naming her current emotional state, disgust. Samantha had to admit and own that disgust is what she was feeling. It was not too challenging for her to do that. The next piece, however, was far more difficult. I reminded her that if she chose to continue holding the emotional pattern of disgust, then she would be driving forward their relationship with that emotion. That emotional state was already causing her to veer far off course from the vision she had for their relationship. Change in this relationship could not happen until she aligned her emotional state and approached her spouse from a lens of acceptance. I pointed out that her state of disgust around Jeff was not only impacting Jeff, it was also impacting their daughters and her.

I shared, "The pain you often feel in a circumstance that you have tolerated is because you have diminished yourself. If somebody chooses to diminish themselves and other people, what can you do about that? What can you do to stop them from doing it? If he chooses to diminish himself, what can you do to stop him?"

From the position of trying to change Jeff, Samantha lost all her power. She had to accept that it was okay for him to do whatever he was choosing to do, for him. He might continue to choose to do those things forever. She had to get to a place where she could accept that reality. She had to recognize what she was choosing to do in the relationship and could no longer blame him for it. She had to check where she was deferring accountability through blame and was feeling sorry for herself. It was time for her to step back into ownership and enter a new emotional pattern.

The choice and change were now back in her ownership. She could move toward her vision or choose less.

We'll revisit Samantha's story in chapter 9, but for now, an important note about acceptance: In the context of this client case study and in future references to "acceptance" in this book, understand that we are not referring to situations where there is abuse or harm being inflicted on another person. Actions to be "accepted" are those that affect only the person taking the action.

Self-Awareness and Centering Yourself

What if you realize you're not aligned in the desired emotion when you're already in a conversation with the other person? This can easily happen when we get a phone call from someone out of the blue or we are busy doing one thing and then find ourselves in conversation with them over a challenging topic. Regardless of how the conversation starts, take a quick assessment of yourself to identify what emotional state you are in.

Let's say you're in conversation with your significant other or a family member and you notice that you are not in a love-based emotion. There are a couple ways you can take a pause and tend your side of the relationship before reconvening. Try one of these phrases to allow yourself the space and time to get aligned:

"At the moment, neither of us is centered. I'd like to request that we take some time, and we'll come back to talk about this."

"I'm going to check in with how I feel when I communicate and listen to you. I need a bit of time and then we can continue this conversation."

This is the time for you to reflect on your vision for the relationship. What is your goal here? You want to make sure you are focused on listening to the other person when they communicate. To make ourselves more receptive and open in listening, I highly encourage you to make the following exercise a regular part of your day. Your nervous system and the other person will thank you!

EXERCISE: Four-Sided Breath Technique

When we're feeling a bit resentful, a bit afraid, or shut down, we know that we are not prepared or ready to take good action. Use the Four-Sided Breath to center yourself. When we can get to a place of acceptance, peace, love, compassion, joy, or inspiration, we can trust the actions we take.

Start by touching your tongue to the roof of your mouth. With your spine straight but relaxed, breathe in through the nose for a count of four. Pause and hold the breath briefly at the top. Exhale through the nose for a count of four. Exhaling through the nose stimulates the vagus nerve which regulates the rest, repair, and digest functions in the body, thereby eliciting an experience of calm in the body. Pause and hold the breath at the bottom.

Once you feel comfortable with this breathing pattern, close your eyes. Doing so will support you in becoming more sensitive and aware of what's happening inside of you. Notice how you feel in your body. Notice if there are areas where you can relax further. Continue to breathe in and out through the nose, focusing on the breath and engaging this same rhythm. Hold a gentle physical smile on your face. Continue this for a few cycles.

Then, as you breathe in, think to yourself, "I am…" As you breathe out, think the word "peace" or any other love-based emotion you wish to activate, such as gratitude, acceptance, compassion, joy, or love. Continue this for a few cycles.

Practice this three to five times a day. It only takes a couple minutes each time. With consistent practice, you will be able to do it with your eyes open as you interact with your life. You will be able to do four-sided breathing when you're at work, interacting with your kids, engaging with your family, or hanging out with your friends.

With consistent practice, you will be able to access a love-based emotion by simply breathing in one to two cycles of the four-sided breath. You can tap into this love-based emotion like a reflex and do it at will. That way, when challenges arise, your body is already prepared and knows how to shift into action in most situations.

There will, however, be times when we cannot get ourselves in an aligned state. In those scenarios, we need to do the best we can when the situation calls for us to do something. We are not always able to pause or center ourselves, especially if we're new to this practice and it is not yet a reflex. Do your best.

But, if you can take some time to get yourself into alignment before you send that text, before you write that email, before you say something or do something, the outcome is much more likely to be aligned with your vision. Alignment will, at the very least, change your experience of the situation.

Remember, nothing stays the same.

CHAPTER 3
EMOTIONS AND ACCOUNTABILITY

*WE DON'T CREATE FROM WHERE WE THINK WE ARE;
WE CREATE FROM WHERE WE ACTUALLY ARE.*

Now that you have the basics of emotional awareness and how to shift your state of being, we need to do a deeper exploration into our emotional capacity and how we can train ourselves to improve our emotional abilities. What I mean by emotional capacity is the ability to become acutely aware and sensitive to what you're feeling and where you are emotionally.

It is important for you to understand that emotional capacity is not some esoteric concept or hippy-dippy "good vibes only" mantra. Our emotions are expressed in a physiological way through our nervous system, not just the creation of a feeling in our minds. The type of emotion, whether expansive or contracting, correlates with different parts of our brains and results in different physical outcomes.

In a research article titled "Autonomic Nervous System Reactivity to Positive and Negative Mood Induction: The Role of Acute Psychological Responses and Frontal Electrocortical Activity," the evidence suggests that "positive emotions (e.g., joy or happiness) elicit differential heart rate (HR), blood pressure, and peripheral vascular resistance responses as compared to negative emotions including anger, fear, and sadness."[4] Our emotions, both expansive and contracting, are our nervous system reacting to the situations in our lives. It's essential that we become emotionally savvy and attuned to our emotional state.

When I take on new clients, the first and most important question I have them ask themselves is, "How do I feel?" It's a question that I have them ask every session for the first full year of working with them. Yes, a full year! Regardless of their previous years of therapy or beliefs around their level of emotional capacity, it takes most clients a full year to really understand the question and answer it accurately. It's a lack of skill, not a lack of willingness to be authentic, and that takes time to develop.

We live in a society that is emotionally illiterate, where we've been told to suppress our emotions or that we're not allowed to feel what we feel because they're "bad" emotions. It doesn't take long to lose our sense of connection to our emotional state. We're not given

---

[4] Kop, Willem J., et al. "Autonomic Nervous System Reactivity to Positive and Negative Mood Induction: The Role of Acute Psychological Responses and Frontal Electrocortical Activity." *Biological Psychology*, U.S. National Library of Medicine, Mar. 2011, pmc.ncbi.nlm.nih.gov/articles/PMC3061260/#:~:text=Positive%20emotions%20also%20result%20in,%2C%20&%20Watkins%2C%201995).

the education and training on how to correctly sense the emotion we're feeling and to acknowledge and name it accurately.

The positive news is that training emotional capacity is doable with time and consistent practice. The most effective way to get proficient at recognizing where you are is checking in on a daily basis. It's developing an awareness and sensitivity of your nervous system, the emotion you're experiencing, and naming your emotional state. Because emotions are tied to our nervous system, their presence affects other psychological processes like attention, cognition, learning, and memory. Our emotions play a key role in our mental health, physical health, and well-being. That's why when we practice these tools to increase our emotional capacity on a regular basis, we're developing the capacity for self-awareness at a whole other level.

Try it right now. Say to yourself, "At this moment, how do I feel?" Just check in. What's the sensation in your nervous system? Can you name the emotion? Am I feeling sad, happy, and joyful? Do I feel regret? Am I feeling angry? I feel shame. I feel guilt. Remember, if you can't yet name the emotion, can you start by identifying whether you're in a contracted energy with your nervous system in fight or flight (related to emotions like anger, jealousy, disgust, etc.), or are you in an expansive energy (related to emotions like compassion, joy, peace, etc.). Simply tune in to where you are.

Do you feel like you were being authentic in your answer about your emotional state? Did your mind try to tell you that you shouldn't feel that way or that you should be feeling a "better" emotion? Did you hear the familiar "things aren't so bad" playing back in your mind if your initial emotional reaction could be perceived as negative? Did your mind try to negotiate with you to feel something different or more positive? I get it. I've been doing this for more than twenty years with myself in an obsessive manner. I still don't have it down perfectly. I do it way better than I used to, but I still sometimes miss the mark. Sometimes I'm just frustrated with where I am and I don't want to acknowledge it even to myself. But then I ask myself who I'm hurting by not being honest. The answer is me.

GETTING CONNECTED TO OURSELVES

In this book, this process of identifying our emotional state is an exercise of one. Nobody is judging whatever emotion is first to come to mind. Remember when I said that only *perfect* practice makes perfect? This is one area where you can start to retrain yourself to be more authentic and connected with yourself and what you are actually feeling. It's not easy though, which is why people spend month after month working with me to shift some of the deep, unconscious patterning that leaves them stuck.

Recognize that there is no benefit to convincing yourself that you're someone you're not. The danger in not being connected with ourselves is that we're setting ourselves up to never achieve our vision. Who you think you are or want to portray does not change who you actually are and the energy you are bringing to each relationship. Energy never lies.

Have you ever been frustrated with your significant other, but you want to come across as "the bigger person" so you pretend you are fine or unbothered? It doesn't matter what you say or how you appear to show up, you will still be in the energy of the emotion you are actually feeling…and your significant other will know that. They have an energetic connection to you and will still sense your emotional energy, whether you're owning up to it or not. The same thing happens when you're feeling sad, but you put on a smile around your friends. You may look happy to them. You can even talk about happy things and laugh together, but they will be able to sense that something is off.

When your words and facial expressions don't match your emotional energy, it creates a challenge for the other person to effectively listen to the words you're saying because they're receiving mixed signals from you. This only creates further communication breakdown in relationships, which is why we'll be spending a significant amount of time talking about communication in the next section of the book, "The Relationship."

A report by the Heart Math Institute (HMI) found that when people are in close proximity, their heart and brain fields transfer electromagnetic energy from one person to another. HeartMath Institute Director of Research Rollin McCraty explains, "The heart generates the largest electromagnetic field in the body. The electrical field as measured in an electrocardiogram (ECG) is about 60 times greater in amplitude than the brain waves recorded in an electroencephalogram (EEG)."[5]

This field is found to have electromagnetic information or coding. More fascinating, however, is that HMI identified that "intentionally generated positive emotions can change this information/coding." What that means is that our emotional state not only impacts our electromagnetic energy, but it also has an impact on those around us. No matter what expression your face has, your electromagnetic field won't lie about your real feelings.

Remember, we're not here to turn you into a better actor. We are here to make you a better person. Acting as though you're not in a

---

5 "The Energetic Heart Is Unfolding." *HeartMath Institute*, 26 Mar. 2015, www.heartmath.org/articles-of-the-heart/science-of-the-heart/the-energetic-heart-is-unfolding/.

certain emotional energy will not change the situation. Instead, it will put the unspoken reality smack dab in the middle of the relationship. It creates that "elephant in the room" and eventually you'll have to address it. When there are repeated energetic emotional mismatches over time, it destroys trust and often destroys the relationship. To have better, vibrant relationships you must be authentic with where you are.

One common argument I hear from people doing the work is that they can't improve their relationship if the other person lacks emotional capacity and awareness and always says that they're "fine". People may feel frustration when it seems that they're the one doing all of the work and the other person continues to show up as themselves–and not in an authentic way.

Aside from gifting them a copy of this book for every holiday season until they agree to read it, there is little you can do when they continue to describe their state as "fine".

Remember, you can't control them, just as you would not appreciate it if they tried to exert control over you. Instead, you can show up in the emotional energy of empathy and compassion. You can also let go of your expectation that you will impact their mood or change their behavior. Doing so is a gift to yourself. You are releasing yourself from an impossible task–making the other person do exactly what you want. You are gifting yourself an emotional energy that feels better to you and keeps you aligned with your vision. Always keep that vision in sight.

Train Yourself to Be Mindful of What You Create
Relationships can expand and grow or contract and decline. Nothing stays the same. This is important to acknowledge because it means

that the way your relationship is now is not how it will be in the future. It's like coming to a fork in the road and having to choose between going left or right. You get to make the choice of what direction you want to head in, and you do that by deciding how you want to show up.

Let's think about this another way. Chances are you're reading this because you have a relationship in your life that matters to you and that you want to make better. You may currently have feelings of anger, frustration, or resentment toward the other person. If you choose to not change and remain in this same emotional state, where do you think your relationship will be in five years? Will it stay the same? Of course not! You are already angry, frustrated, or resentful. Adding additional years of that may not cause the other person to change at all, but it will create a change in you…and not for the better.

Now consider the alternative. You are in your current state of anger, frustration, or resentment, and you consciously choose to train yourself to show up in a different energy over the next five years. Where will your relationship be in the future? It's hard to say. We can't say for certain how the other person will respond, but you are giving them the best odds to show up better for you. You will be in a completely different emotional energy, which will give you a new perspective on your relationship and help you see whether it is evolving in a way that aligns with your vision. It empowers you to choose the future that you continue to create, and you're doing it in a way that honors yourself.

Try saying this out loud and see how it feels: "It doesn't matter what the other person does. I really can feel how I choose to feel. What the other person is doing doesn't have to define how I feel.

They can do what they're going to do. I can choose how I'm going to feel about it."

There's a lot of power in this.

HOW WE DECEIVE OURSELVES

You may have read up to this point so far and thought to yourself, "Okay, I can do this. I take ownership of my emotional energy and I will no longer try to control the other person." Great! The challenge is that we don't always realize or recognize when we're trying to control or manipulate another person, as it's been taught to us in a way that appears to be kind or sympathetic. We'll say things like, "I'd like to be more patient with my partner."

Let's look at that more closely. You want to be patient. You want to do good by giving time and space to your partner. What are you giving them the time and space to do? That's right—change themselves! You want your action (a Doing) to hopefully change what they are doing. Does that ever really work though? In the meantime, you are carrying an emotional energy (your Being) that may be something like frustration at their current behavior. If you are patiently waiting in a frustrated energy, you are doing little to help yourself and nothing that will have a real, positive impact on the other person.

These phrases we tell ourselves have the power to easily convince us that our patience is something that does good. I'm not saying to throw patience in the trash, but if you do not tend to the underlying emotional pattern of frustration, you are likely to end up carrying it around for quite some time. Instead, if you tend to the frustration, it's likely that something new will occur.

This is why one of the most common phrases I hear from couples when they're at a major inflection point in their relationship, like a divorce, is, "I don't know how we got here!" They thought they were doing all the right things, but they never actually changed their emotional state of being. At some point, one partner reaches their breaking point and either leaves or initiates a divorce. The other person is often left confused, not entirely understanding why their partner left. How does that happen in relationships where people have often been together for years if not decades? Sometimes people even comment, "I thought we were good," or, "I haven't done anything differently for the past nine years."

You can get away with almost anything once. You can get upset. You can say some things you don't mean. You can almost always get away with it one time, and sometimes even two or three times. But, if you get upset and you say hurtful things week after week, month after month, year after year, things don't stay the same. Bit by bit, the emotional energy you're bringing will continue to wear away at the relationship until it hits its breaking point. Then, the other person changes their behavior because of the energy you're bringing, and they either have an affair or they leave you.

The Other Person Is Not Responsible for Your Emotions

Some people believe that if they have a relationship they will be free from the emotional pattern of loneliness or insecurity. They rely on the relationship to foster or enhance positive emotional patterns within them. In fact, I would say that somewhere between 80 to 90 percent of clients I work with who have engaged in a romantic relationship did so hoping it would solve something for them. People may also seek to be freed from feelings of loneliness or insecurity by having a child.

Unfortunately, these situations often create a bigger problem. The other person can't actually change those emotional patterns within you. The only person who can shift feelings of loneliness or insecurity, as an example, is yourself. Only when you own the emotional pattern of loneliness and insecurity within yourself and take responsibility for shifting it, can you actually have the experience of security and connection within the relationship. Death to any relationship, even before it begins, is to make the other person or the relationship responsible for shifting a feeling within yourself.

Take a moment to think about a prior relationship you had that did not work out. Do you remember the circumstances around why you entered into that relationship? What was your emotional state prior to the relationship beginning? What was your motivation for entering into the relationship? If you were not in a love-based emotional pattern (not craving love, but already experiencing the emotional state of love within you), then you may have set up that relationship to fail. Unconsciously, you may have been looking for a relationship to solve for a pattern of fear, insecurity, or loneliness you were carrying. Unfortunately, when we look to a relationship to solve our inner emotional challenges, it rarely ends well.

SETTING UP RELATIONSHIPS TO THRIVE

Let's look at what we can do instead to enter relationships in a healthy way so that they have a better chance of thriving. What emotional energy do you think would be important to bring with you into a relationship? If emotions like confidence, love, compassion, joy, or inspiration come to mind, then you are learning fast!

If I'm already feeling inspired, already feeling love, or already feeling a sense of connection before I enter a relationship, then I am not relying on the relationship or the other person to provide something to me. Instead, I'm looking at the relationship as a way to simply share myself with another person or to enhance the life I already have.

There are a few ways in which a relationship can enhance our love-based emotional state. Take love for example. Many people are taught to believe the whole point of a romantic relationship is to feel loved. Somehow the relationship itself is supposed to be the generator of the feelings of love you have. People want to manifest love as if it's some elusive, external emotion that they will be allowed to claim once they find their significant other. That's not how love works.

As with every other emotion we've discussed so far, you must learn to foster love within yourself, as yourself, first. Once you can do that, you possess the emotional energy of love that you can then give to the other person. If you don't know how to find love and recognize love within yourself, how are you going to give it to the other person? You can't.

Now, if you and your partner both understand how to foster love within yourselves, that becomes a beautiful thing. That's where the phrase "in love" comes from. It's not that you're feeling love because you met your soulmate or the only person in the entire world that you are meant to be with. You are both "in love" because you each showed up with an emotional energy of love.

Let's look at the emotional energy of adventure. That is a feeling we can foster within ourselves and that a relationship with a friend could also enhance. If your friend shares a similar energy and prioritizes adventure, you may find yourself taking more hikes, traveling to new places, and trying new things. You hold the emotional pattern of adventure, and your relationship fosters and supports that.

Trust is the same. We can hold trust within ourselves. It's something a relationship with someone like a business partner could support. If we line up with the right person, someone who aligns with what trust means to us, the business relationship absolutely could enhance and support trust. We can experience the same when it comes to the emotion of intimacy in romantic relationships. Your relationship with your significant other may support your sense of intimacy.

What are emotional patterns that you can carry that a relationship could enhance? Write them down. You might say something like, "I am responsible for love first. The relationship can enhance it second," or, "I am responsible for joy first. The relationship can enhance it second."

THE EMOTIONS YOU PUT INTO A RELATIONSHIP

There is another way you can explore and check in on your emotional state, which will help you realize what type of emotional energy you are putting into your relationships. The first thing to do is to answer to the emotional experience within yourself. For example, if you wake up every morning feeling shut down and angry, you'll answer to that every day as the experience of your life, regardless of what the other people in your life do.

Second, you have to answer to your emotional state and your impact on other people. When you hold onto something within yourself, it becomes a pattern within you. At some level, it impacts your family, your friends, your colleagues, and other people in your life. Nothing is an isolated event when it comes to inner patterns.

Third, you must answer to the way people respond to you. At some point in time, maybe your friend says to themselves, "I don't need to hear all that negativity right now." You often won't know what they are thinking, but they'll demonstrate it through canceling plans or distancing themselves. This is extra important if you have children. They often learn about themselves by what you teach them and the examples you set. If they see you shut down or angry in relation to their other parent, they may copy you by shutting down and getting angry as a way to manage their relationships with others.

When it comes to a dynamic you wish to change, you need to make it important. You need to make it real. That's what allows it to change. If you bring the importance of what you want to teach your children to the forefront, it will no longer be acceptable to shut down and be angry.

You're going to see that you can completely redefine how you see and interact with your relationships, now and forever, if you choose to do it. It doesn't have to take years. It doesn't have to take months. It can happen now.

Growing Your Emotional Awareness

As you develop greater awareness, you'll begin to see that there is conscious action you can take, and your perception of relationships will shift. For example, say your friend is having a bad day. Perhaps they treat you poorly or they act passive-aggressively. In the past you may have been inclined to match their emotional energy, but now you have the awareness that your emotional response is yours to choose. With enough training and practice, you will be able to stop, take a few breaths, and think to yourself, "Oh, they're having a bad day. This has nothing to do with me. I choose to be compassionate and joyful regardless of how they're showing up."

That may sound basic and simple. However, it is a basic simple skill very few people possess. When we get into a routine with the people we're close with, it's even less likely we have that ability and capacity. This is because we have trained a way of being together and it's become a very fast reaction. It has become a reflex.

We all know people who go through the world seeming perpetually pissed off. They speak aggressively. They're critical of others, and they blame constantly. When they're interacting with someone in a customer-facing role, they're often rude and don't usually receive the best outcome, just the outcome they've bullied out of the person. If it's over the phone, they might get spontaneously "disconnected" from customer service, making things even worse for themselves and inflaming their fear-based, "negative" emotional state.

The interesting thing is that often these people do not realize that they have created their own state of being, and they continually add fuel to the fire. They point to examples of how people treat them and bad situations that happen to them as the reason they're in their bad moods. They might feel mad that people in their social circles aren't supportive or that nobody seems to help them out. They often do not realize that they take themselves (and their energy) wherever they go, and that is why life seems to continue to present them with challenges.

Life doesn't have to be such a challenge. Imagine that scenario but in the exact opposite. Imagine a person who regularly shows up with a sense of compassion, joy, or kindness. As a general impact, most people around that person are going to feel safe. They may even want to go above and beyond to help that person or connect with them. People are attracted to them and desire relationships with them. Situations often get resolved more peacefully and respectfully because the person has shown up in an emotionally expansive state. Imagine how nice that life could be!

If you can easily envision an emotionally contracted person and see how situations play out in the world for them, can you also see how an emotionally expansive person's situations can play out in the opposite way? It's okay if you're not there yet. The more you train your own emotional awareness and control, the clearer it will become. You will start to see example after example of how your love-based emotional frequency creates an expanded influence on others. It will make you wonder why anyone chooses to live in a constant fear-based emotional frequency.

Once you train this emotional capacity you improve at identifying where you are and what tools you need to use to change things. We have greater freedom to choose when we want to change and when we don't. The reality is that even in mastering this knowledge, we will not always be in an expansive energetic frequency. I still have moments when I catch myself in a bad mood and find myself saying, "Joey, you absolutely know how to shift and change this for yourself, and you're just not doing it. And, you know the result of that is stupid pain. You are causing and perpetuating that pain." Most times that snaps me out of it, but sometimes it doesn't. It's then that I say, "Yep, I'm just gonna pitch a fit." We all have our human moments. The point is with this education, we become the ones who can decide how we show up!

BECOMING ACCOUNTABLE

Intensity has long been a part of my life. While some intensity, like the chaotic energy of my childhood home, did not seem to serve me in a beneficial way, other intensity, like from my martial arts instructors, helped me develop a rigorous and driven work ethic that has allowed me to grow and evolve at a rapid pace. They held me accountable for my words and actions, so I grew to do the same for myself.

In one encounter with one of my super intense martial arts instructors, he called me over and said, "Joey, do you know what I am?" Panic swept through me. I was used to what felt like "trick questions" from him, and not knowing the answer to the unanswerable questions was often painful. With great apprehension, I responded, "No, sir. Sorry, sir." We stood in awkward silence as I waited for either his verbal or physical response.

"Joey, I am an ax." Oh boy, this was probably going to hurt. He continued, "Do you understand what that means?"

"No, sir," I replied.

He said, "I'm an ax and you're a tree, and I will chop you down whenever you need it."

I responded, "Do I need chopping, sir?" hoping that the answer would be no.

"Not right now," he said, "but just know that's who I am for you."

While the words were moderately terrifying at first, I am grateful to this day for the role he played in my life. He fulfilled that statement, too. Whenever I would get full of myself, he would metaphorically cut me down to size.

If I was doing something wrong that was hurting somebody else, he was there. If my behavior wasn't beneficial to a situation, he let me know. And when he was no longer physically present in my life, I became my own ax to keep my words and behaviors in check.

A NEW UNDERSTANDING OF ACCOUNTABILITY

We often think of accountability as a responsibility to do something or show up in a certain way. I would like you to suspend that definition for the time being and think about accountability in a new light. The truth is you are always accountable to something. In the context of this book, you are accountable to showing up for your vision, or you are accountable for choosing something else. For the sake of differentiation, I refer to this as accountability (showing up for your vision) and deferred accountability (choosing something else). You are still *always* accountable to something.

When it comes to the training in this book, I invite you to be more rigorous with yourself than you have ever been. Maybe even more rigorous than anybody else will ever be with you. This relationship you're working on has to matter so much that it feels like your life is on the line. In many ways, it is.

What you can train yourself to do here and in this first relationship you've chosen to work on, you will bring to all your other relationships. Your life will quickly start to shift and gain speed exponentially in the direction of your vision. Your life as you know it will fundamentally change, and you get to decide in which direction you'll go.

When I train people at a high level, I know they often have a 50-50 shot at achieving their vision. They have a 50 percent shot at hating me and deciding that this is not for them. They have a 50 percent shot that they have a breakthrough in their life, that it will become unrecognizable from how it was before. Why? Because I won't let them off the hook. They must be accountable. I won't entertain their stories and excuses as ways to defer accountability. I'm not going to let them live where they are if it's not creating the thing they said they wanted for themselves. If they are as rigorous with themselves as I'm willing to be with them, their life will be unrecognizable. This is something we have to train.

Be your own ax. Chop the things down that aren't going to create what you want. Chop the things down within your space and then burn them—these ways of being will never get the result you want for yourself. It's not about the other person first. First and foremost, it's about you.

Ways We Defer Accountability

We can never be without accountability. We're either accountable to our vision or we're deferring accountability away from it. You are still always accountable, and the direction you're headed is your responsibility.

If you're not accustomed to taking responsibility for your actions or being incredibly honest with yourself, accountability may be a struggle for you. It is for many people, and there are three primary ways that I've found people defer accountability: blaming, feeling sorry for themselves, and having no belief.

Blame happens all the time—it's when we make ourselves, another person, or the world responsible for anything that is not how we want it in our lives. Feeling sad? It's your spouse's fault. Struggling in your career? It's because you should know better and keep making the same mistakes. Didn't win the local election in your town? It's because the system is rigged.

In each case, we defer accountability by pointing to an external factor that we deem responsible for who we are or what our life is like. But guess what—blame doesn't do anything but keep you stuck in contracted emotional patterning.

It's also easy to want to feel sorry for ourselves in the hope that it will provide us temporary relief and better feelings about our current situation. A person using this type of deferred accountability often takes on the role of victim or has a "poor me" mentality. They believe that life is happening to them as if they are merely a passenger to their own lived experiences.

Having no belief is a common way to defer accountability because it relies on a lack of vision, which many people do not take the time to create. There are several ways that people defer accountability through no belief. It may sound something like, "They're not willing to change," or, "They're always going to be this way." No belief can also be about us when we say things like, "There's absolutely nothing I can do," "I am who I am," "I'm too old," "I'm too uneducated," or "I'm not pretty enough." We may not believe in others' ability to make positive changes, or we may not believe in our own.

In each of these three situations, you may find yourself entering into an internal negotiation to try and substantiate why you're deferring accountability. You may think to yourself, "They're being terrible to me, and I am not being nearly as terrible to them. So, the way I'm behaving is totally okay and justified." Any time you catch yourself justifying your own poor behavior, you're placing yourself as superior and less egregious. My martial arts master would ax that behavior in a second!

I've also seen people (myself included) who substantiate not being kind because the other person is not kind. We enter this "you go first" mentality of believing that the other person has to or should make the first move before we can respond with a beneficial, expansive emotional energy. The problem is, when we follow this tactic, we refuse to examine ourselves and change. In doing so, we defer obtaining our vision for the relationship.

This is why we start this entire book focusing on you first. You are not making this shift in your life for someone else. You're doing it for yourself. If you don't hold space for the intention you want to fulfill in your relationship, who's going to do it? No one. Often, the other person doesn't know what you want them to do or how to do it. You are now learning the "how" in making this personal and life shift.

Client Example: Deferring Accountability through No Belief
I was going through my mail recently and found a letter from a woman named Hannah who participated in my Evolution program a while back. I remembered that she came to me because she was in a relationship with a man named Mike who was highly addicted to

drugs and alcohol. Hannah herself had once been highly addicted too, but she desired to change and signed up for Evolution.

After Evolution, Hannah took accountability for her life and did the work to get sober. She was no longer using, but Mike still was. It was a highly abusive situation, and she believed that Mike would never change. She was falling into no belief, deferring accountability for the relationship she hoped to preserve. She couldn't see a way that it was possible.

I said to her, "Your partner is not choosing to change for now. They're not changing yet." I added, "You don't get to pick if they're going to change or not. That's not your responsibility." Hannah realized that she could continue to opt into this harmful relationship or she could choose to show up differently. She invited Mike to move out, which may have taken Mike by surprise given that she had never shown up that way before.

Hannah shared in her letter that as a result of her own personal transformation and movement toward vision, Mike finally had the eye-opening moment he needed to quit drinking and drug use. Mike sobered up, too. Hannah shared with me that she made the decision to opt into the new and evolved relationship they now had. Neither of them has engaged in the addiction behavior for many months, and they now have a completely different relationship. You just don't know when people are going to choose something different for themselves. But you can opt out with no belief.

Accountability Self-Assessment

Check in with yourself after reading that last section on deferred accountability. What methods do you find yourself using in your current relationship? Nearly everyone (or at least nearly everyone who has yet to go through one of my programs), uses blame, feeling sorry, or having no belief to try and explain why they're in the situation they're in.

Use this time to get honest with yourself and be your own ax. Are you blaming yourself, others, the world, your workplace, or someone or something else for where you are? Check in and ask if you're feeling sorry for yourself. Are you playing the "poor me" role? Or do you need to return back to your vision so that you can move out of the "no belief" method of staying stuck in your relationship? It's okay to identify it. You are learning how to empower yourself in ways that few people will ever get the chance to. Be clear on that.

One of the best ways I know to get over our own deferred accountability is to own it. You need to take the time to get real with yourself and recognize, "Hey, I'm deferring accountability by way of blaming," or, "I'm deferring accountability by feeling sorry for myself," or, "I'm deferring accountability right now by having no belief." That is the quickest way I know to own something for myself. Acknowledge to yourself what it is that you're doing.

If you are reading this book, you have a chance few people ever have. There are a lot of people who want to change their lives, and they don't have the tools. They don't have the training on how. You can definitely learn how to stop deferring accountability. The point of giving you this information is so that you can recognize when you're doing just that. Pay attention to what you are about to create. Stop, redirect, and realign.

Once you declare it, you can't stop there. You have to really own it. "At this moment, this is how I'm feeling. I am responsible for how I feel. I deserve better. They deserve better from me." Then you can make a commitment to do better. If you essentially own it in this way, you'll be able to let it go.

There is freedom and acceptance in acknowledging where we are and in giving ourselves permission to shift... or not. Accept that you're here in this current state and relationship. It's okay to be where you are emotionally, and it's okay to make a shift. There's both acceptance and permission. For example, I could accept that I'm feeling sad and then decide to just feel sad. "I accept that I'm feeling sad. It's okay that I'm feeling sad, and I'm choosing to feel that way."

The other option of acceptance and permission approaches the emotion differently. It says, "Okay, I'm feeling sad. I wish it were different right now, and that's all right." But it doesn't stop there. It goes on to say, "I'm giving myself permission to step out of the feeling of sadness and go somewhere else." In the acceptance and permission to shift it, we change ourselves.

You can't just go through the motions of saying it to yourself and have it shift. You've got to decide that it's important and actually go into it with commitment. If all you have access to is just saying it first, that's okay—start there. We have lots of tools for how to get to the place of willingness to give ourselves permission to truly own the emotional state we are in.

One of the strongest ways to give yourself permission is to acknowledge it to yourself. You need to acknowledge that if you continue to show up in a pattern of sadness, for example, then you will continue to take a certain action and it will have an impact on your relationship. You're basically saying, "If I put *this* into a relationship, here is what I am going to get out of it."

On the other hand, if you consciously choose to change it, what could it mean for your relationship? Imagine a few of the possibilities.

Consider what might occur if you choose to change. This helps to give us permission to be accountable to ourselves. If you desire a new relationship, accountability is crucial.

CHAPTER 4
SETTING EXPECTATIONS FOR YOURSELF

UNFULFILLED EXPECTATIONS ARE THE CAUSE OF PAIN AND SUFFERING IN RELATIONSHIPS.

You have your vision. You know the emotional energy you want to bring to your relationship. You commit to being accountable to yourself. Now, it's time to get clear on what you expect from your relationship with the other person. This isn't a laundry list of demands with which you hope the other person will comply. Our expectations are the bar we set for ourselves, not how we will manage or manipulate the other person.

When you think about a recent conflict or difficulty in your relationship, you will likely find an unfulfilled expectation at the root of that conflict. Unfulfilled expectations typically fall into one of two categories: something was supposed to happen but didn't, or something happened that wasn't supposed to. There's a subtle but important distinction here—it's either the absence of something that was expected or the presence of something undesirable to us.

Similarly, fulfilled expectations fall into one of two categories: something happened that was supposed to happen, or something didn't happen that wasn't supposed to happen. Again, there's a similar distinction—the thing we wanted is present, or the thing we don't want is absent.

In order to get clear on our expectations for the relationship, we must first get clear on our needs, wants, and desires.

UNDERSTANDING YOUR EXPECTATIONS

How comfortable are you feeling with the material so far? This entire section has been focused on you and the ways you can transform your relationship through creating a vision, sharpening your emotional awareness and skills, and taking accountability for your circumstances. I would advise you not to enter into this final section until you feel comfortable and confident in these other areas.

While you're certainly welcome to read through this section, if you attempt to implement it before you've nailed your side of the relationship and practiced maintaining love-based emotions as much as possible, you will not have the impact you desire in your relationship. In my many years of experience across many client situations, I have found that if you enter the realm of needs, wants, and desires *before* you are in an aligned state, your requests of the other person become absurd. You cannot ask for respect or love if you are in the energy of anger. You cannot ask the other person to show up with compassion if you are aligned with fear. You can only name how you'd like the other person to show up if you yourself are in an emotional state that is aligned with your vision.

WHAT ARE YOUR NEEDS?

We're going to name the things that may be the easiest to identify—our needs, or the non-negotiables, of our relationship. We all have non-negotiables in every type of relationship. We all have deal-breakers. Another way to think about non-negotiables is needs that are so crucial, if they are not met, the relationship will end.

Our non-negotiables will vary greatly depending on the type of relationship we're focusing on. The non-negotiables we hold in a romantic relationship are very different from the non-negotiables we have in a business partnership. As an example, I am absolutely okay with my employees dating around. I am definitely not okay with my wife dating around.

I run a business and have needs from my employees. I am clear on what those needs are. If they don't show up to meet those needs, what do you think happens? They get fired. When a non-negotiable isn't met in this context, our relationship evolves. However, even among business owners, the needs may vary. At one business, the need might be that the employees show up on time for work or that they clock in a certain number of hours per week. Their need might be a minimum sales quota or that they demonstrate proficiency with regularity.

Because each relationship and each person is different, your needs list in one relationship will not look the same as your needs from another person. Even people who are in the same types of relationships, like a romantic relationship, may have very different needs lists because their visions are not exactly the same. Let's figure out what matters to you.

EXERCISE: Define Your Needs

Begin by writing down whatever you believe your needs—or non-negotiables—are in the relationship you've chosen to work on for this book. Think about the person you are working with. Ask yourself, "What do I expect from my significant other, my business partner, my friend, or my child?"

If you think you don't have any needs from your children, look deeper. Do you need them to sleep at night so you can function during the day? Do you need them to stop destroying your belongings or leaving the house without permission? We absolutely have needs in every relationship, even with our children. I promise the needs are there.

If you're not entirely sure if something is a true need of yours, write it down anyway. People often think of things as "needs" that don't actually belong in this category. That's absolutely okay, and we'll sort that out later. For now, just write!

WHAT'S A REASONABLE NEED?

Now that you've had time to think about it, let's expand our understanding of what needs actually are. If you struggled with the previous exercise, that's okay. Most people have no idea what their personal needs are in a relationship. This is where relationships can break down so quickly, because if you don't know what your needs are, it's nearly impossible to communicate them to the other person. When one person doesn't communicate their needs, it doesn't mean that they don't have them, it just means that they're not clear on them. And whenever you have true needs for your relationship that aren't being expressed or met, you may find yourself in patterns of frustration, anger, or resentment.

Naming your needs enables you to communicate them to the other person. If you don't name them, the other person cannot know what they are. (Remember my ex-girlfriend who thought she "needed" one phone call a day to help her insecurity, and then even when that happened, she was upset? The one phone call was not actually a need for her.)

You may find that you have needs in a relationship and that the other person isn't able to show up for them for one reason or another. You keep wanting or expecting them to meet a need, but they never do. What is the problem? It may be that your expectation of them is unreasonable. Whether we do it intentionally or not, there are times when we have expectations that the other person cannot meet.

To clarify, a need is simply an expectation. Remember, when something is truly a need for us in a particular relationship, that need must be met or the relationship will end. For example, monogamy is a common need in many romantic relationships. Unlike needs, our wants are expectations we would *like* to have met in a relationship, but if the person cannot or will not meet expectations around a want, we can either evolve the expectation with our partner or get it met by another person. A want in your friendship relationship may be something like doing yoga together. Both our needs and our wants set an expectation for the relationship.

Let's look at what four criteria must all be present in order to consider an expectation reasonable.

A Reasonable Expectation:
1. The other person clearly understands the expectation.
2. The other person is willing to fulfill the expectation.
3. The other person is capable of fulfilling the expectation.
4. The expectation aligns with my vision for this relationship.

Let's look at the first criterion, that the other person clearly understands what is expected of them. I'm sure you've been in a relationship before when a person asked you to do one thing but really wanted something else. When you did it the way they said instead of the way they envisioned in their mind, how did they respond? Chances are they expressed some sort of dissatisfaction or frustration. You may have noticed yourself responding with a similar energy because you thought you were doing what they needed, but they really needed something else. Not having a clear understanding of the expectation is setting the other person up for failure. The chance of a need getting met increases 90% simply by knowing you have the need and telling the other person that it exists.

The second criterion is that they're *willing* to fulfill the expectation. Sometimes one person's expectation creates a significant burden on the other person, making them unwilling to fulfill it. Looking back at the story of my ex-girlfriend, if her expectation had been that I call her at 7 p.m. on the dot every night when I was in the middle of my martial arts training, I would not have been willing to rearrange my schedule to fulfill her expectation. I was open to connect with her at other times, but if 7 p.m. was a non-negotiable time for her, I never would have been willing to meet that need.

The third criterion is that the other person is *capable* of fulfilling the expectation. If you demand that your partner quit smoking and go "cold turkey," are they capable of doing that? If you want your roommate to now make dinner every other night even though they don't even know how to boil water, you are asking them to do something they don't yet have the skill set for. You either have to allow time for them to gain that skill set (if they're even open to doing so) or seek a more reasonable expectation (like having them order dinner, start with take-and-bake meals from the grocery store, or chip in money for you to cook).

The fourth criterion is that what you're asking of the other person is aligned with your vision. We're not discussing our non-negotiables with the outcome of seeing how much control we can exert over the other person or how much we can get them to opt in to. Sometimes people's desire for power or control causes them to start requesting more and more from the other person as "needs" when actually the requests have nothing to do with the vision for the relationship. In these cases, it can actually end up sabotaging a relationship that was headed in the right direction.

Gaining Clarity on Reasonable Expectations

If you're a little stuck and you're battling with whether your needs are reasonable or not, there are a couple ways to clarify. Is what you wish to communicate actionable, meaning the other person can do something about it? Is your expression of what you need clear and specific, or could someone interpret the request in more than one way?

For example, a common need communicated among romantic couples might be the need to feel desired. I hear this often, and people are surprised to learn that this is *not* a reasonable expectation. First of all, what does "feeling desired" even mean? You could try and explain it, but the other person may still not understand how to show up for you on that one. What may make one person feel desired, like routine physical touch, might be a turn-off for the other person if they were hoping for expressions of desire through flowers or thoughtfully written notes.

People can define their need for feeling desired further by clarifying with statements like, "I need to hear words of affection from you. Please tell me that I'm beautiful and share with me how you feel." Or maybe it's, "I need to hear you say 'I love you' and that you care about me." Even when it comes to a need to feel desired by physical touch, it's important to clarify, "I need you to touch me. I need you to hold my hand. I need you to hug me."

If you express only a general need to feel desired, you are looking to the other person to make you feel a certain way without being clear on what that means or looks like for you, and the lack of clarity is what makes this need unreasonable. Remember, we can't control another person's feelings, but we can control our actions. It works the other way, too. Someone else can't make you feel desired, but they can take actions that are meaningful to you and signal desire. If your need from the other person is a feeling that you want them to create in you, you have an unrealistic expectation. You are saying that you are no longer responsible for how you feel, and we've already established why it is problematic for you to not take ownership of your emotions. As soon as you go there, you've set up an impossible situation.

NEEDS VERSUS WANTS VERSUS DESIRES

To put it simply, our **needs** are our non-negotiable expectations for a relationship. The relationship cannot continue without these things.

Our **wants** are the things that are important to us but are not deal-breakers if they don't happen. Our **desires** are like the cherry on top of the relationship—if they happen, it's great. They're things we enjoy or that make us feel good in the relationship, but their absence does not create painful feelings.

Maybe you've already realized that some of the items on your needs list aren't actual needs in order for your relationship to function and be aligned with your vision. It doesn't mean that item doesn't have value or importance to you, it may just mean it belongs in a different category. Our needs are the things that must happen in the relationship in order to continue forward in an aligned way. Even if your needs don't occur to you right now, my hope is that they will be more apparent to you by the end of this book.

As you're going about your day, pay attention and notice when disappointment shows up. Is that pointing to a need for you? Is what the other person is doing non-negotiable in your relationship? If it's not, then you've probably happened upon a want or desire. Make note of these, as they still matter to you in the relationship, but they aren't deal-breakers associated with your needs. You may also notice a need you've had for a while that has gone unmet. If that's the case, what used to be a need may actually be more of a want now. You have decided that you are okay existing in the relationship whether that want is met or not.

Is It Really a Need?

Let's look at the list you created in the last exercise and further evaluate each one of the things you wrote down. The question to ask yourself for each is, "Is this truly a *non-negotiable* need?"

The word *non-negotiable* means one of two things:

1. If that need goes unmet, the relationship will end immediately.

2. The relationship will only survive a short time without the need being met. A short time means weeks, not months or years. You may end the relationship by never speaking to the person again, or the relationship evolves into something else.

If you think about each need on your list and it doesn't meet one of the two non-negotiable criteria, it's not a need. It's most likely a want. You may have listed things you thought were needs but are actually wants, meaning you have strong feelings about them, but they are not deal-breakers in the relationship.

Say one of your needs in a friendship is kindness through words and actions. If your friend is unkind for a day or two, that's usually not a deal-breaker. If they continue to be unkind for a long period of time, then the relationship may end. Kindness in that friendship meets the criteria of a non-negotiable need.

For your romantic partnership, monogamy may be a need for you. However, even monogamy can mean different things to different people. For some people that may mean no sex with another person outside of the relationship. For others, that includes no porn.

Monogamy may be a non-negotiable need for you. You know that if you found your partner was sleeping with another person, that would end the marriage for you. However, there are other people who, if their spouse were to have an affair, would try to work it out. If that is you, then monogamy is not a need for you, it's a want.

You may also realize along the way that some things you thought were needs don't actually serve you or move you toward your vision for the relationship. I worked with a mom whose "need" was that her daughter brush her teeth every day. She considered it a need because of the importance of dental hygiene and not wanting her daughter to get cavities. For whatever reason, the daughter didn't want to brush. It was causing the mom a lot of suffering and stress. The more the mom seemed to stress and try to force her daughter, the more the daughter resisted. The mom was losing her mind at the idea of this apparent need not being met. She came to realize that this was not a useful need for her. When she took the pressure off herself and her daughter, changed her emotional energy, and looked at it as a want, things got better for both of them.

Wants and Desires

Once you're clear on what your true needs are, everything else on your list becomes a want or a desire. Go through your list and write "need" next to your non-negotiables.

Then write "want" next to anything that is really important to you. A want is something you have strong feelings about but isn't a deal-breaker. It's really important that the other person in the relationship shows up for the wants, but if they don't, you'd find another way to get that want met. The relationship still continues.

Your desires may be anything on the list that remains. You may have desires that didn't even make the list because they're things that would be nice to experience in the relationship, like a shared interest in hiking or love of vacationing in Paris, but you wouldn't be unhappy if they're not present.

Some needs will be present in a number of your relationships, while some will not. Most of us tolerate behavior from family members that we would never allow from a friend. If a friend behaved like a certain family member did, we would end that friendship. In my own life, I have different needs for my brothers than I do for my friends. There are behaviors I tolerate from my brothers that would be a deal-breaker in my friendships. Why? Because my vision for each relationship and what I want out of it is different. All the relationship visions are aligned with my life vision, but each relationship vision has its own expectations. Every relationship requires and has different needs.

Why It's Important to Say What You Need

Through my trainings and the clients I've worked with, I've found that most individuals don't feel it's okay to have and express needs. For some it feels selfish or like they're creating an ultimatum (we'll get to those later on in the book). So they stay silent. They absolutely have needs, everyone does, but they let those needs go unspoken year after year.

The needs never go away, and unfortunately their needs not being met deteriorates the relationship until the point that the person often lashes out in a horrific way. Their words are often fueled by anger and resentment. This is when people demand a divorce or end a friendship and it feels like it came out of the blue. The other person never saw it coming because they didn't realize what expectation they weren't upholding in the relationship.

Accept that you have needs and that you need to evaluate them. Are they healthy? Healthy needs align with the vision you're looking to create. Just because I say I have a need, that doesn't automatically mean it should get met. If it's not aligned with my vision, I'm looking to make something happen that isn't even really what I want. Interestingly enough, it's a mistake that people regularly make. Not everything that feels like a need to you is for your greatest good. Not everything that feels like a need right now in your life is going to move you toward your vision for your relationship.

Once you've determined what your needs are, if they're reasonable, and if they're healthy, it's time to communicate the need. We'll be focusing on communication as one of the tools in the next section of the book, "The Relationship." We'll also discuss how to express needs, set boundaries, and train and reinforce these processes so we can bring everything together. For now, accept that within any relationship, you have needs.

CONCLUSION: WORKING ON OURSELVES

You've made it this far and have hopefully had several eye-opening or aha moments along the way. Before moving into the next section, be sure that you are clear on your vision for life, your vision for the relationship, and your expectations.

Name your feelings every single day. Continue to train yourself with techniques like the Four-Sided Breath and moderating your emotional state. It's essential that you commit to your emotional training, creating routines until they become reflexes. That is why I created the Power Series, which includes Power of Emotion, to deepen your emotional awareness and capacity. You can find more information in the Resources section of this book.

You'll notice that there are some repeating themes in the remaining sections of the book, and that is by design. We need to approach these concepts from several angles, working through them again and again, until their existence becomes a part of our lives. We need to change the way in which we move through the world and then watch as the world opens up for us!

PART 2
THE RELATIONSHIP

CHAPTER 5
UNDERSTANDING THE RELATIONSHIP

YOUR RELATIONSHIP WILL NEVER GROW BEYOND YOU.

When two people are putting energy into one another, it creates this thing called the relationship. Relationships are the inner mixing of all our ways of being with another person's ways of being. This can be a beautiful creation in and of itself. It can also feel like the greatest challenge of our lives. Every single relationship is unique and possesses its own special qualities and challenges.

No person puts the exact same thing into every one of their relationships. This is also why I say no parent has the exact same love for each child. Yes, I know they love their children, but their relationship with each child must be different because each child is different. No child (or other living creature for that matter) shows up the exact same way as another. There is beauty, challenge, and opportunity in that. We get a fresh approach to each of our relationships, and we can choose the ones we welcome into the vision for our life.

Additionally, relationships are unique between two individuals and can experience dramatic shifts due to the pattern dynamics and relationship dynamics present. As we discussed in the previous section, our energetic state impacts and influences the relationship. Imagine the relationship dynamic in which both parties show up with a state of anger and righteousness. Imagine how that same relationship might present differently if one person shows up with anger and righteousness, but the other is in a state of compassion and appreciation.

In this section we'll focus on how energies come together. The relationship is like an energetic ecosystem. You define what *you* want to contribute. The other person defines what *they* want to contribute. We'll explore what our own expectations should be around control in the relationship, how to communicate our needs, wants, and desires, and how to set healthy boundaries to establish an aligned connection between ourselves and the other person. This is the next big step in your journey toward a vibrant life.

RELATIONSHIPS THROUGH THE LENS OF VISION

By now, we have a clear vision for our lives. We know what we're looking for in terms of our health, wealth, relationships, lifestyle, and intimacy. We understand that there are energies that move us toward our vision and energies that move us toward something else.

Take a moment to close your eyes right now and think of your vision. See yourself in it and all of the wonderful things you will be, do, and have in this aligned place. Notice where you might feel it in your body and the emotions that arise when you sit in your vision. Name your emotional state. Carry it with you as you read on.

At the beginning of this book, you selected one relationship that you wanted to work on. Ask yourself what the purpose is of this relationship. Why do you want to be connected to this person?

Let's say the purpose of your relationship is friendship. What is your vision for this friendship? If you desire friendship, who do you need to be in the relationship in order to fulfill the vision for friendship? That's right. Even though we're focusing on the relationship as a whole, we will always come back to you.

Even if you desire a friendship with this person and it's part of your vision, the other person has the choice whether to show up for it or not. You cannot control whether they opt in or opt out. That's not your responsibility, and quite frankly, not even an option for you to decide. Instead, what you *can* do is align yourself with the vision you have for friendship and pay attention to those who are willing and capable of showing up for it.

It's also important to evaluate your expectations through the vision and purpose of the specific relationship. What you expect of your business partner should be very different from what you expect from your children; your expectations of your siblings are different from your expectations of your friends. If you need to revisit what you wrote down in the previous section about your non-negotiable needs, wants, and desires, you can do so now.

Every one of the relationships in our lives is meant to fulfill something regarding our vision. We have different relationships in our lives for a reason. Friendships fulfill different things than acquaintances. You may have a handful of close friends and have a set of expectations for them. You may have twenty or fifty acquaintances with a very different set of expectations in those relationships. You have colleagues with whom you often spend more time than you do with your family. The relationships you have with colleagues support specific things in your vision for life.

There are expectations in business relationships that differ from those of friends or acquaintances. There are a multitude of family relationships, from parents to children, to siblings, to extended family, in-laws, and deceased or estranged relatives. Each of these relationships has its own set of expectations and supports specific aspects of vision. Finally, you may have or want a romantic relationship, which supports multiple areas of your vision for life and has its own set of expectations.

We did a great deal of groundwork earlier to define our vision for one particular relationship by identifying the Being, Doing, and Having aspects of that vision. Bring that vision back to mind as we explore this second aspect of the relationship—the relationship itself.

CONTROL AND THE RELATIONSHIP

Who doesn't love to be controlled in a relationship, right? I'm joking, of course. Nobody has ever come to one of my seminars wanting to be controlled; it's always the other way around. They want to be free from feeling manipulated or pressured to live in a way that is not aligned with what they want from life. What they often don't realize, though, is that they actually aren't being controlled—they're being *influenced*, whether it's in a way they like or dislike, and up until this point they have chosen to opt in.

You can *influence* the other person and the relationship. Influence is different from control. Influence is you showing up in a certain way and with a certain emotional pattern, and the other person chooses how they respond to the way you're showing up. Control is forcing someone to do something against their will.

Client Case Study: Control versus Influence

I had a client named Jess who worked in an office for a temperamental boss. The more upset he seemed to be with her, the more she would shrink into her shell and apologize, even for things that weren't her fault. She was nearly at her breaking point and considering quitting her job. She even had a dream that her boss yelled at her and she packed up her things in a fit of rage and stormed out.

But she didn't want to do that. She enjoyed the work and many of her coworkers. Her position was aligned with her vision for life, but her boss's energy left her feeling depleted. I asked what Jess needed from her boss and she said, "Respect." I asked her what that looked like and she said, "Acknowledging my work for what it is rather than passing blame. Refraining from unkind words and raising his voice." We talked Jess through the energetic pattern she would like to be in, which was compassion, and how she might show up differently for future interactions.

Jess wrote to me months later to share that she had recently been promoted at work, something that was also a part of her vision for career and wealth. She explained that after training with me, she returned to her job and had the opportunity to test her skills immediately. Her boss was livid over an apparent audit error and slammed his fist down on her desk, spilling her coffee in the process.

Using the Four-Sided Breath technique and other tools I taught her, she shifted herself into the energy of compassion. For the first time, she stood up from her desk, looked him in the eye, and said,

"I understand that you care very much about this company. I do too and I want us to be successful. If you'd like, I'd be happy to walk you through why this is not a big issue and show you how our team followed protocol on this. Perhaps now would be a good time to reevaluate our protocols."

She said her boss looked shocked and then got quiet. He walked away but returned with some paper towels to clean up the coffee mess while asking her if she could explain to him what happened. Before their meeting, he even went and grabbed her a new cup of coffee from the breakroom. Jess said she remained calm and in the energy of compassion throughout the meeting, and as a result, her boss was open and receptive to listening to her. The experience opened his eyes to the quality of her work and her level of care. And when promotion time rolled around a few months later, her name was top of mind.

Taking Responsibility for Your Side of the Relationship

You are responsible for the four things you put into the relationship—your emotions, thoughts, words, and actions. If you bring sadness to the relationship day after day, that has a particular influence on the relationship. If you bring joy, on the other hand, that has a radically different influence. At the end of the day, the relationship cannot grow beyond you. That means if you cannot manage yourself well, your relationships will suffer. If you can grow into a passionate, loving, courageous, inspired person, your relationships will thrive. The more you grow, the more your relationships will grow.

That is why I've developed the Power Series curriculum, which is explained in the Resources section of this book and is available online at innermatrixsystems.com. Power of Focus trains us in managing and directing the mind and thought strategies. Power of Emotion trains the ability to manage and determine the emotions we feel and how we respond to the world around us. Power of Vision trains us in the tools and strategies of creation and the actions we take. Power of Intuition trains the capability of the "how," developing our ability to leverage intuition to bridge the gap from where we are to where we want to be. We should never stop growing.

What's Within Your Control

I do not want to create the assumption that control is something "bad" or "evil." Taking control of what you can and should control is incredibly empowering. Tapping into your ability to recognize what you can control and choosing to take control of the course of your life is what I wish for you and everyone else.

You can 100 percent build yourself into the person who has the relationships to which you aspire. You can control what you do and how you respond to the people and world around you. You can design and grow into the person you choose to become. You can hold your vision for the relationship you want to create and hold yourself accountable for taking actions that lead toward your vision. You can determine the *what*. You cannot determine the *who*.

Your responsibility is yourself, everything you put into the relationship, and ensuring that it aligns with your vision. From there, know that you can influence but not control what the other person does or how they respond. You can manage your expectations of the relationship and the other person in a way that your vision gets met. You can also manage your expectations of the relationship and the other person in a way that diminishes and breaks the relationship down.

There is so much that you can control in your life, but that control is all related to you and not the other person or the relationship. It doesn't matter if you think your control over them will help make their life better. It doesn't matter if you think controlling the relationship will bring about the best outcome for everyone. Control yourself and see how others respond.

What If the Other Person Does Not Seem Willing to Grow?
One of the most common concerns I hear from people earlier on in their relationship training is along the lines of, "I'm growing, but my partner isn't. What should I do?" The fear is that they're doing all of this work, but everything around them or the relationship they wish to heal will still remain the same. What can we do if the other person does not seem to be doing the work as well?

If you are reading this book and you're interested in personal development, or if someone you're in a relationship with invited you to read this book, you're clearly here and willing to develop yourself in some capacity. If you're a person who is constantly growing as a human being but you're in a relationship with somebody who does not share your passion for growth, don't pressure them. You'll be about as successful as if you tried to get a pet pig to sit and watch a football game with you. I know that example may seem absurd, but you're hoping for an outcome that they have no interest in and may lack the skill set to perform.

Instead, allow them to be where they are. Just make sure two things are in place as you grow, change, and evolve:

1. They support who you are and who you're becoming.
2. They have a decent ability to be with themselves.

For the first point, examine if the other person is encouraging your growth. Are they supportive of you changing, or do they complain? If you find that more often than not they whine and say things like, "Why are you leaving again? Why are you changing? I don't like it," that's no good. If you're growing and they're supportive of it, that's great!

The second piece is whether they can be without you or not. If part of your personal growth includes traveling or hanging out with friends more, that's okay, as long as your partner is self-reliant. If they can manage themselves while you're out there growing, you're good. Keep growing and just allow them to be who they are and appreciate them.

In some cases, though, your needs might change, and this person may not be willing or capable to meet those needs. In that case, it's time to transition the relationship. But, don't *start* there.

If you're with somebody who isn't on a path of growth in the same way you are, that's totally okay. Be patient. The work you're doing will influence them (and yourself) in a way that will either evolve the relationship to grow or evolve the relationship to end. You'll find that the more you continue to move toward your vision, the more people you'll attract to your life who also align with that vision and, ultimately, will be supportive of your unlimited potential for life-long growth.

CHAPTER 6
DEFINING BOUNDARIES

BOUNDARIES ARE THE WAY WE UPHOLD EXPECTATIONS.

Talking about boundaries seems to be all the rage nowadays in social media and self-help circles. Don't get me wrong, boundaries *are* incredibly important, and I'm glad so many are having conversations about it. At the same time, we need to have the *right* conversations about boundaries to understand how they work for us and can leave both parties in a relationship in a healthier state. Boundaries should not be thought of like a line in the sand or a wall of protection that you build. Boundaries are the container for your expectations to be met.

In order to set boundaries well, you must have developed some capacity with the other skills we've covered thus far. You've got to manage yourself and your emotions. You must have a vision for the relationship. You must regularly align with that vision and be aware of what you're bringing to the relationship. From there, you will be able to set boundaries in the relationship.

UNDERSTANDING BOUNDARIES

Boundaries are really just the way we uphold our expectations. That's what a boundary is—a clear expectation about how you need a person to show up with you. If you've already evaluated that your expectation is reasonable and aligned with your vision, then it can be communicated with boundaries.

That means that once you've articulated and clarified the expectation to the other person, you also make sure they are willing to show up for it. We're going to uphold boundaries around needs differently than wants or desires. Like our needs, boundaries are non-negotiable. If you allow a boundary to be negotiated, you have not actually set a boundary. When you share a non-negotiable need and set a boundary, it should be communicated as such.

The other person has the decision to opt in or opt out of your needs and boundaries. In some cases, they might say, "No, I'm not willing to show up for that." You then decide how to respond. If it truly was a non-negotiable need for you, it may mean that the relationship is incompatible with your vision for life and needs to change or end. Others discover that what they thought was a need is actually a want. If it's a want, it would be beneficial for you to realize that you're actually okay with it not getting met. That realization will save you great suffering.

When They Won't Honor Your Boundaries

What about when you have a need and the other person won't honor your boundary? I hear this often from people who say, "Joey, I set a boundary and they're not respecting it!" They go on to describe how their partner ignored or violated the boundary ten, fifteen, or twenty times. Oftentimes, their partner continues to tell them they're *going to* show up for the request, they just didn't that time for one excuse or another.

The optimistic person then commits fully again to the relationship only to have the partner not show up the way they promised they would. Some people ask me, "How long do I allow for that need to not get met before I make a change?" Often the underlying hope is that somehow, they can honor their vision and get their needs met without actually having to address the boundary violation or change the relationship.

For most people, it takes time to change their habits. There are few people who can learn of someone else's needs and boundaries and say, "Yep, I'm going to change that right away!" and they wake up the next day and it's done. In fact, almost nobody can do that. Change is an inevitable part of life, but change doesn't always happen as soon as we want.

You want to make sure there's an evolution of positive change in the relationship over time. That starts with naming the amount of time that would make sense to see a positive evolution. Each situation is different, though. If the change relates to something that's a need for you or makes you unsafe, you may need to seek change in a short time frame.

One way that you can achieve change in a short time is by choosing to complete the relationship and move on. It's important that you understand that nine times out of ten a relationship can thrive with the steps in this book, but that leaves one out of ten relationships that can't. Ending a relationship should never be done as a knee-jerk reaction. This is particularly important because ending the relationship may not be aligned with your vision or get you to the place you want to be. Boundary setting, changing your level of engagement, and communication (all ideas we'll discuss here shortly) may help you get the relationship back on track.

If you're considering moving on from a relationship, consider first doing the following:

1. Set a time frame that you will be all-in with your vision for the relationship. Give yourself a reasonable period of time in which you actively work on improving the situation.

2. Evaluate what unfolds in the relationship during that time frame. Did you make some progress? Do you need more time to assess?

3. Determine whether the nature of the relationship supports your vision; if it doesn't, accept that something needs to change.

4. Evaluate the new level of engagement you would like to have in the relationship.

In the rare case that you do move on, it doesn't mean that you've terminated the relationship indefinitely. You can choose to remain open to reuniting in case the other person eventually decides to change and show up the way you need. This may simply be an adjustment to your level of engagement with the other person. We'll discuss levels of engagement more later in this chapter.

CONDITIONS FOR BOUNDARY SETTING

As with the previous conditions we've discussed for us to be successful in our relationship work, boundary setting has its own set of conditions that, if followed, will support you in establishing healthy boundaries that align with your vision for your relationship. Remember—when you uphold a boundary, you are upholding your vision.

The following four conditions are required for boundary setting:

1. **Clear Ask.** You must make a clear and specific request that the other person understands.

2. **Opt In.** The other person must choose to opt in for your request.

3. **Ability to Enforce the Boundary.** You must be *able* to follow through with the boundary.

4. **Willingness to Enforce the Boundary.** You must be *willing* to enforce the boundary.

Client Case Study: Boundary Setting

Jim was one of my clients and wanted to work on repairing his relationship with his longtime friend. Jim expressed his frustration to me that his friend was often late to things, including to the airport for a trip they planned together. Jim felt disrespected and upset by his friend's apparent lack of concern for time or the plans they made.

Jim identified that timeliness was a need of his for this relationship. His vision for life involved traveling and going on adventures with friends, so he needed to know that the friends he chose to be in his life were also showing up in a way that supported his vision. He didn't know if this friend would be on board with setting boundaries around time.

He started by setting a time boundary for their next meetup at a restaurant. Jim told his friend, "I enjoy hanging out with you, but it's important to me that when we make time for each other, you're on time. So when we have dinner tomorrow at 6 p.m., I am asking that you arrive on time. If you're not there by 6:05 p.m., I will leave the restaurant."

Jim's boundary was 6:05 p.m. Jim's friend had a clear understanding of the expectation with a definitive boundary. His friend had the option to opt in to Jim's need or opt out. Jim decided to enforce the boundary by leaving the restaurant if his friend did not show up by 6:05 p.m. Fortunately, due to Jim's clear communication on what he needed from the friendship and why, his friend made it to dinner on time for the first time ever. Now they are both accountable for upholding their vision of the relationship and continuing the friendship for years to come.

BOUNDARIES AND LEVELS OF ENGAGEMENT

When boundaries are adhered to or violated, it may change our level of engagement in the relationship. The level of engagement you put into a relationship will have an influence on you. This is different from the other person having an influence on you.

As I've said before, you cannot manage the other person's actions or energy. You can manage the influence the relationship has on you. We do this by determining our level of engagement with the relationship—engaging more with the relationships that align with our vision and less with the relationships that don't.

As a quick example, let's say I have a friend I enjoy hanging out with but they're perpetually late to things. My level of engagement with them will depend on the type of activity I'm doing and how much of a desire I have for them to be there on time. If I buy great seats for a concert, I will not be inviting them to join me, as they most likely won't meet my expectations to be on time.

There are relationships in our lives that leave us feeling inspired and hopeful and those that leave us feeling cynical and anxious. Pay attention to the impact of all your relationships. There are relationships you engage in where you're more likely to have a few drinks and stay out later than you normally would, and others where you're more likely to hike up a mountain and have a nutritious meal. It's important to evaluate how much time to spend in various relationships through the lens of your vision for life and your vision for the particular relationship.

Depending on how the relationship aligns with your vision, you can determine your level of engagement in the relationship as:

- No engagement
- Low engagement
- Medium engagement
- High engagement

For me, there are individuals in my past who were abusive. They were violent, called me names, and put me down. Regardless of whether they were family or longtime friends, I chose the "no engagement" level for these relationships.

Examples of low engagement relationships would be the people in your network or family with whom you may not be close, but you may spend time with around the holidays or other events. You'll be in medium engagement with many friends, family members, and likely your adult children, whom you may connect with on a more regular basis, maybe only once or a few times a week.

High-engagement relationships are most often those with your significant other, your young children, your close colleagues, and close friends. These are our daily interactions, often for many hours of our day. These relationships have a significant influence on us.

When we view our relationships through these lenses of engagement level and vision, we begin to realize which relationships we're focusing on too heavily that are keeping us from our vision and which relationships we may need to engage with more to move us toward it.

Determine your level of engagement by the degree to which a relationship supports and nurtures your vision for life and enriches your level of fulfillment. Also, understand that your engagement level is likely to ebb and flow depending on where your focus is. You may be in a sprint in your career or business, so you may be in high engagement with business partners and colleagues and in low engagement with your significant other and close friends for a time. If we stay aligned with our overall life vision, the engagement level of our relationships will support us for what we need and where we're headed in each stage of life.

EXERCISE: Engagement in Your Relationship

Having awareness of our level of engagement in a relationship can help illuminate where we may be directing too much of our emotional energy or where we're not directing enough. Perhaps you're here to work on your romantic relationship, but you realize it's been at a low engagement level for years due to your high engagement level with your business partner and career.

Take a moment to consider the following:

1. How would you describe your current engagement level for the relationship you chose to work on for this book?
    a. No engagement
    b. Low engagement
    c. Medium engagement
    d. High engagement

2. What level of engagement in this relationship would move you in the direction of your vision?

3. What actions might you need to take to change your level of engagement in this relationship so that it moves you in the direction of your vision?

CHAPTER 7
COMMUNICATION

JUST BECAUSE WORDS ARE BEING SPOKEN, DOESN'T MEAN COMMUNICATION IS TAKING PLACE.

Have you ever had someone talk *at* you instead of *to* you? They don't care to engage in a conversation and probably care little if you're comprehending what they're saying. They word-vomit all over you and then seem satisfied that they said their piece. While they may have felt like they were communicating, they were not engaged in communication (and, honestly, they would have had better luck had they talked to a wall).

Communication is one of the most common relationship challenges. I could spend an entire book just refining communication. Many people come to me understanding the importance of communication and seeking to improve it but lack the skills and practice to do so. One thing I hear often is, "Joey, my partner and I just need to talk more." The reality is that they usually need to talk less, at least in the beginning.

If the way you've been communicating with each other is ineffective, adding more time and more words will not improve the situation. In fact, it often makes things worse. More words and time will seldom improve the emotional energy of the conversation. If you were calling each other names or taking passive-aggressive jabs in your short conversations, a longer conversation will often just result in more names and more jabs.

When it comes to relationship communication, the goal is not to talk more, it's to talk more effectively.

COMMUNICATION FRAMEWORK

When you're communicating with another person there are four important things that need to happen in order for the communication to be effective:

1. Communicating clearly and specifically in a way the other person can understand.

2. Confirming the other person understands your communication.

3. Actively listening to their response.

4. Sharing with them what you heard to confirm your understanding of their response.

Likewise, when you're receiving communication, there are four important things that need to be present:

1. Actively listening to what's being communicated.

2. Confirming your understanding of their communication.

3. Responding to their communication.

4. Confirming their understanding of your response.

I realize this may sound like a lot to do in a conversation at first. With practice over time, it will feel natural and conversational to actively listen, confirm, and respond to each other.

Think of it this way. When communicating, I have to deliver a package—I have to communicate what I intend to say in a way that the other person can hear it. Once I have communicated and delivered the package, I need to make sure that the other person received the package and understands what was intended. I've got to make sure that the box isn't all banged up, that the glass isn't shattered inside, and that it was received correctly. From there, I need to make sure they respond to my communication. Finally, I need to make sure I understand their response in the way they intended it. That cycle repeats itself.

Consider this hypothetical script to illustrate the process.

Jill: I need to have an important conversation with you. Are you open to that?

Jack: Sure.

Jill: *(Step 1: Communicating clearly and specifically in a way the other person can understand.)* Ever since we moved in together, I have been enjoying spending more time with you. At the same time, I am finding that I no longer have enough alone time for myself. I know that you love when we do activities together, like grocery shopping and going to the gym. I do too. However, I think I need to start doing some of these things on my own. Does that make sense?

Jack: So you're saying you don't want me to go to the gym with you?

Jill: *(Step 2: Confirming the other person understands your communication.)* Sometimes I would enjoy going to the gym by myself, but not always. There may be different ways during the week that I want to spend time by myself.

Jack: Okay, that makes sense. How will I know when you need alone time?

Jill: *(Step 3: Actively listening to their response.)* Would it be okay if I communicate to you before I go and do a thing, to let you know if I want to do it alone or together?

Jack: I would appreciate it if you could give me as much notice as possible so that I can plan my day accordingly.

Jill: *(Step 4: Sharing with them what you heard to confirm your understanding of their response.)* Of course. I hear you saying that you'd like to know what activities I would like to do together and what I would like to do by myself so that you can also plan your day and activities. Is that correct?

Jack: Yes, that would be helpful.

Even though this may feel very structured, for the time being, it is necessary to practice this until it becomes a reflex. Eventually, it will feel more conversational. Take it slowly at first and make sure you are hitting each of the steps when speaking or listening. As you get better at communication, communication becomes a conversational exchange. Consistently check in and make sure that the four parts of the communication framework are happening perpetually.

I find that often, people try to skip out on the clarification and confirmation pieces of the conversation. This is not a place to cut corners and is actually where things often go awry, even when both people earnestly want to connect around a need or want. If you confirm that the other person understands and opts in, you're much more likely to hit the mark together.

If you find you're not aligned in your understanding, go back and evaluate your communication to see where the breakdown occurred. This doesn't have to happen immediately during the conversation. In fact, some may assume that alignment has occurred as a result of the communication only to realize days or weeks later that a breakdown did indeed occur and the person is not following through with their agreed-upon action.

You can approach the other person and say, "Hey, maybe I either misspoke or perhaps you misunderstood me. Did we talk about [topic]? Can you please share with me what you thought was supposed to occur?"

There are two possible outcomes. The other person may incorrectly share back what they thought you said, in which case you need to clarify your communication, or you'll discover that they did understand, but something got in the way of their follow-through. If it's the latter, you'll need an entirely different conversation to understand what the barrier to their follow-through was.

Lastly, it's important to note that this communication framework applies to all communication, not just conversations. The same rules apply if you're texting or emailing. Just because you send an email and you believe you've been clear does not mean that the recipient understood it the way you intended. You can ask them what they understand your request to be and confirm that it was received correctly. With practice, this will become more conversational. Repeat, repeat, repeat.

Listening

Think about the number of times someone was speaking to you and you were busy formulating in your mind what to say next or how to respond. You have an answer or a rebuttal even before the other person stops talking. When we do this, we are not hearing anything and are instead prioritizing our desire to be heard over listening to the other person. A bit ironic, isn't it?

This can be especially true around "hot topics" in any relationship. The moment one person mentions a particular topic, the other person may assume they are going to hear the same thing they "have heard a hundred times." But when we stop listening, we miss the opportunity to hear where there may have been growth or change in the other person. We're operating from the assumption that this is going to be the same old communication, so we produce the same tired result: a miss in communication.

Active listening is the opposite. When we are actively listening, we are present and absorbing each piece of information the other person feels necessary to share with us. Being in an active listening state allows us to pick up on more details and cues of what they're really trying to say rather than defaulting to our brain's favorite hobby of filling in the blanks.

Active listening allows us to have more meaningful and productive conversations aligned with our vision. If you're reading this book, you're doing so because you want to improve a relationship in your life, right? It is virtually impossible to improve the relationship with the other person if you are not willing to take the time and make the effort to actively listen to them. There are no shortcuts here. You need to train yourself to slow down and take in what they're saying before you formulate a response.

I've found that people seem to struggle most with this either because they want to jump to whatever response will show that they're "right," or because they are uncomfortable with silence. In active listening, you take in what the other person is saying and then confirm your understanding. This must happen before you make any additions to the conversation or share your perspective.

Let them know that you have heard and understand what they are saying. Once you've done that, you may need to take a brief pause to collect your thoughts on how to respond. This can be a challenge for people who are uncomfortable with silence and feel the need to take up airspace. Learn to get comfortable with silence. Oftentimes it won't take nearly as long as it feels to you and creates valuable space for you to make sure you're still in the emotional frequency you want to speak from before you speak.

"Joey, let me make sure I have this straight. You mean that I have to listen, check in on my nervous system and emotions, make sure it aligns with my vision, *and* create a response?!" Yes. It might feel clunky at first, but it is something you will become fluent in with enough practice, repetition, and patience. And if you're not willing to take the time to practice until you reach fluency, what is your alternative? The exact same relationships you've been experiencing all along.

Do the work. It's worth it.

NAVIGATING HOW THE OTHER PERSON COMMUNICATES

"But Joey, what if the other person does not want to communicate with me using these tools? Why do I have to be the one to do all the work?" First, let's not make the assumption that the other person doesn't want to learn and grow in this way. The reality is that most people want to work toward being a better version of themselves. If you're telling yourself that they are not willing to do the work, you're just speaking from your assumption.

If you apply what you are learning in this book, especially aligning your emotional space with your vision of the relationship, perhaps it will occur to you to line up with the other person in a different way. What I mean by that is that using the tools you've learned means you are already showing up differently to them. The relationship is already experiencing a shift. So, the same exact results from the other person is less likely because they are now being presented with a new situation.

You may be able to show up in a way that makes the invitation feel different to the other person, and that might influence them more toward opting in. What we can do is really dial in our side of it first, and then make sure that when they are available, we relate to them differently. Never underestimate the power of relating to someone differently, even if you're not in direct communication with them.

Client Case Study: Communicating When Estranged
Janel was the mother of a daughter who was in college. The two women had not spoken to each other in almost two years. Janel's daughter refused to come home for holidays or family events and essentially cut contact with her mom. In Janel's mind, the relationship was broken and had no hope for repair if she couldn't have a conversation with her daughter.

I asked Janel to first focus her attention on what she did know and could assess in the relationship. I said, "When you think about your daughter, how do you feel?" Janel took a moment to tap into her nervous system and emotions and discovered that there was some resentment there. She sat with it a bit longer and felt disappointment and sadness. These were the energetic frequencies that she was bringing to the relationship, whether they were in contact and communicating or not.

I reminded Janel that she could indeed work on the relationship by tending to those things that she had the ability to tend to—her emotions. I asked her what emotional energy she wanted to be in with her daughter and which energies would align with her vision for the relationship. She said she desired to feel love and compassion. It was her work now to think about her daughter while holding the frequency of love and compassion.

Within a week of Janel holding this energetic state within herself, her daughter unexpectedly called. This time when they had their conversation, her daughter got a very different response than she would normally get from Janel. Rather than feelings of resentment, disappointment, and sadness, Janel showed up with love and compassion. This started a new trend in their relationship.

Today Janel and all three of her daughters get along very well. In fact, they all took a trip to Hawaii together and are all part of each other's lives. They're interacting more harmoniously, simply because Janel made the decision and did the work to manage her emotional space.

At first glance, it may not seem like this is enough, but trust me when I say, it's everything.

When the Other Person Won't Respond

There are situations, though they are the exception, in which the other person will either not respond at all or they will not respond differently than they always have. Janel could have shown up with compassion and love and her daughter still could have decided to opt out of the relationship. It would not have been Janel's desired outcome, but it still would have been an improvement in the relationship. Why?

It would still have been okay because Janel, and you, are free. You are free to not carry the heavy energy or burden of emotions that don't align with your vision. You are free to choose how you want to feel inside. While that may not change some of your relationships, it will change others.

The reality is that some people don't stay in our lives. I always say you can pick the *what*. You don't get to pick the *who*. You can pick what type of relationship you would like to have. You can pick what type of connection you'd like to have. You can pick what needs you're going to have and how you show up and have those needs met. You just don't get to pick who's going to meet them—family or not.

WHEN WE MISS THE MARK

Realizing that you're missing the mark is an extraordinary accomplishment. Seriously. Most people never realize when they miss the mark and therefore just keep missing it over and over again and wondering why things aren't working out the way they'd like.

There are times when a person isn't willing to hear what you have to say. Sometimes when you're talking with somebody, it becomes apparent that they are not in a place of listening or genuinely desiring to understand. Regardless of how well you're communicating, the emotional state you're holding, how you're delivering the message, and how often you've checked in for their understanding, some people simply shut down. They may be angry or afraid and are not in a place to listen.

It's not your job to get them to listen. If the other person can't or won't listen and is unable to receive your communication, the only option is to acknowledge it. The best thing to do in that circumstance might be to disengage and come back to it another time and try again. You might say something like, "It seems to me that you do not understand what I'm trying to communicate right now. Let's come back to it another time."

Case Study: Communicating with Children

Lori is a mother who was struggling to communicate with her nine-year-old daughter. When Lori would speak to her, the daughter seemed to shut down and close herself off from communication. In her session with me Lori asked, "How do I make her listen to me?" She was concerned that she was reinforcing behaviors in her daughter that would further strain communication in the future.

Communication with children is slightly different than communicating with adults in that it is our role as adults to teach boundaries and guidelines. I encouraged Lori to be very direct and clear in her communication with her daughter in these moments and say, "I will stay here in this room with you until you're ready to share what is going on." Then I recommended she make eye contact with her daughter and continue this eye contact, all while holding an energetic frequency of compassion and love.

With young children, it's all about training and education. I told Lori that if her daughter persisted, she could add more context by saying, "Listen, I hear you're hurting. It's not an excuse to act out or misbehave. These things are still not okay. I'm here when you would like support and help." Lori's role as a parent is to educate and train.

PRACTICING COMMUNICATING IN YOUR RELATIONSHIPS

It can take a lifetime to master the art of communication. I'm providing tools that you can train and practice to continually improve your own skills, as I continually work to improve mine. Communication is something you're going to constantly work to get better at.

Be mindful of three things:

1. Communicate with consideration of your audience and what their capacity might be, being mindful of what you intend for them to hear.

2. Confirm that the person heard and received your message.

3. Confirm that their understanding of what you communicated matches your intention.

In a general conversation, especially if the other person is not engaged in the same training as outlined in this book, that sequence described above might not make sense to the other person. However, you can still practice being mindful with yourself. It will increase your awareness and help you realize any time the other person doesn't understand, whether they realize it or not.

When you can identify when a delivery doesn't happen, you can continue to refine it. Maybe eventually you get a head nod or another response from the other person that indicates they understand. You can even ask them what they understood. When communicating with someone about a challenging subject, it may be beneficial to sit down and make sure each of these steps is taking place.

Following this framework will provide each person the time to identify, own, tend, and shift their emotional patterns. This will enable you to truly hear one another and make sure you're not just talking *at* each other. Consider practicing this with people who have a common language, such as other readers of this book, for example. With practice, you can enter into a conversation and the process becomes more natural and fluid.

Following the framework optimizes the effectiveness of your communication. This takes practice, like any skill worth developing. So, if you feel like this is a little challenging, that's good. Communication is something you have to constantly work on to improve, and in a lifetime maybe you'll master it. The results in your relationships will be worth it!

CHAPTER 8
SABOTAGING AND SAVING THE RELATIONSHIP

*IF YOU DO WHAT YOU'VE ALWAYS DONE,
YOU'LL GET WHAT YOU'VE ALWAYS GOTTEN.*

You may have picked up this book or had it recommended to you because a relationship has ended in your life. We've all experienced this. The reasons why relationships end usually fit into one of these two categories: the relationship ended because it wasn't aligned with your vision or because you compromised your vision in an effort to maintain the relationship. Either way, the result goes back to you—do you choose what you want out of life or do you move away from vision and face the consequences of people and relationships in your life that don't feel aligned with you?

There are ways that we may sabotage our relationships in an effort to keep them. People often come to me because they or the other person has tried to implement one of three sabotage strategies. At the end of the day, each sabotage strategy is an attempt to make the other person change instead of taking responsibility for your own emotional state.

Conversely, there are tools we can implement to attempt to influence your relationships and not compromise your vision. When I talk about not compromising your relationship vision, I do not mean being inflexible in the relationship. I mean you should not compromise on your needs and vision. When you do, you move away from your vision.

Here are ways that people may attempt to sabotage relationships and what we can do instead.

DON'T USE THREATS AND ULTIMATUMS

Maybe it's because it feels like the ultimate power move to some people, or they're in such a state of desperation, that threats and ultimatums seem like the only step they can take. Regardless of the motivation, threats and ultimatums don't work when it comes to building vision-focused, vibrant relationships in your life.

Don't threaten to fire your employees. Don't threaten to end your friendship. Don't threaten divorce. If you threaten to end a relationship, it's only a matter of time before it ends. Even if you're dissatisfied with a relationship and it may make sense to transition a relationship, don't threaten to end it until you're ready to end it. Threats of this sort tend to shut the other person down. Threats and ultimatums, by their nature, make the other person feel unsafe. Is that the emotional state you want them to have? Is that the emotional state aligned with a vibrant relationship?

Under no circumstances, unless you are prepared to leave, should you threaten the end of the relationship. This is a way to whittle it down. Threats and ultimatums are the best way I know to break down trust with the other person and have them feel highly insecure over time by way of your influence and impact. It occurs to the other person that they can't rely on you to be there, and it reinforces the belief that it's just a matter of time before you leave.

If you threaten the end of the relationship, the other person begins to prepare themselves for when it will happen. That starts to soak into their unconscious thoughts, and they may ruminate on ideas like, "I need to be prepared for when they leave." The other person may not even consciously realize it, but their unconscious mind does. Because of that, there's no way the other person will ever be all in.

The other person will start showing up defensively. They may start opting out with you as a way to prepare for when you leave. You told them, over and over again. One of the most destructive things you can do when you're in a relationship, especially if this is your "go to" when you're upset, is to say, "I just don't think this is going to work." I get that you may feel hurt and scared. But, if we stop and look at the impact of communication, you're basically saying to the person, "You're not worth the effort." You're basically telling the other person it's going to end.

It's important to clarify that a threat or ultimatum is different than a non-negotiable, and you need to make that clear in your communications with the other person. You could say something like, "I've been thinking about this. It's extremely important to me. If you're not willing to show up for this expectation, then I don't know that this relationship will continue the way it is." You haven't threatened the end of the relationship. You let them know what it is they can do in order for the relationship to work. You've also let them know that if things don't change, it may not.

Let's look at an example of a non-negotiable from my own life and how to communicate it in a manner that is not threatening or an ultimatum. At this point in my life, I'm really clear on two non-negotiable things in the context of a romantic relationship—monogamy is a must, and I don't want to have kids. If the other person is not interested in monogamy or they desire to have children, I know that the relationship will not work out no matter how great of a person they seem to be in every other context.

When the other person shares something that seems counter to our needs or non-negotiables, it might send us into a brief state of panic. We might receive it as an unspoken ultimatum, since what they're saying they want is in direct conflict with what we want. For example, if I'm with somebody and she shares that she can't wait for us to have children, I know that I need to take that information, tend to my side of the relationship, and get centered again. I'm going to respond with something like, "I think you're a lovely person, and I really enjoy our time together. I'm really clear that I do not want to have children. It's a non-negotiable for me because of certain things that I've committed to. You absolutely deserve to have kids. If you want that, I'm not your guy. I'm not asking you to change that need for yourself. I think that's great for you to do, if that's what's right for you."

This is not a threat. You're not attempting to manipulate or coerce the other person into changing for you. Instead, you are holding space for them to reflect on their own needs, wants, and desires to determine if the relationship is aligned with their vision.

You are allowing the other person to then stop and evaluate. They may get really clear that children are really important to them and are a need. At that point, we know that we need to transition the relationship. Maybe we will become great friends. There may be a period of disappointment. That's okay. I want to be very clear on that non-negotiable before the person invests any more time with me. But I will not threaten or use an ultimatum to make them change.

Instead, Be All In...with a Time Frame
As you're engaging in a relationship of any kind, be all in. Commit to making the relationship vibrant. Don't be one foot in and one foot out. Either you want this relationship or you don't. If you are feeling uncertain about the relationship or if there are some issues that may not be aligned with your vision, commit to a time frame and then assess whether the relationship aligns with your vision at the end of that time frame. During that period, be all in and confirm that you are tending your part of the relationship in all the ways we've explored up to this point.

Depending on how the relationship may or may not have evolved by the end of your time frame, you will have greater clarity on where you stand and greater perspective on what the relationship is capable of. Be aware though—when your time frame is up, don't treat it simply as an opportunity to just extend the time frame in hopes that something will eventually change or occur. That time frame, with you being all in on the relationship, will show you if the relationship is aligned with your vision or not.

DON'T CRITICIZE OR COMPLAIN

How do you feel when someone criticizes you and names what you're doing wrong? I'm not talking about the "constructive feedback" we may receive at work. Think about a time when someone rattled off a list of criticisms about what you were doing. What emotional state did that put you in? Was it one that's conducive to carrying on a healthy and productive conversation to move the relationship toward vision? Probably not.

Oftentimes when we're criticized or we criticize other people, it triggers a nervous system response of fight, flight, or freeze. When we're critical of someone or they are critical of us, the response may be to argue or slam doors (fight), to go to another room to avoid further interaction (flight), or to shut down and stop interacting (freeze).

These responses make it impossible to positively influence the relationship. Criticizing someone about who they are and how they're acting will not result in the communication you truly desire. If the person is doing something that needs to change, you can name the behavior and the impact it has on you, then invite them to make a change. In doing so, you're focusing your communication on what you need and want for the present and future rather than grumbling over what they did in the past.

At the end of the day, we're all doing our best. We all make mistakes. We all mess things up. When we criticize and complain about people, it breaks the relationship down and has the opposite effect. Instead of striving to be better or evolve, they shut down, run away, hide, and contract.

A similar impact occurs when we complain, even if we're not complaining about the person themselves. If we complain in general, it breaks relationships down. Some people try to do this under the guise of "venting," thinking it will help the relationship in some way. The reality is that it does the opposite.

If you find yourself whining and complaining about the other person, catch yourself and redirect. One of the key things we contribute to any relationship is who we're being—our emotions, thoughts, and words. If the contribution we're making is negativity and complaint, we diminish ourselves, the other person, and the relationship. Complaining doesn't move us toward vision. It's a short-term reaction with detrimental consequences for what we desire long term. Break the habit now!

Instead, Acknowledge and Affirm

How does it feel to you when someone you value says something kind about you or complimentary of you? Good, right? If you're in a relationship that you're working to improve, you need to acknowledge and affirm what the person does well and what you like about them with regularity. Put the majority of your focus and attention on the way the other person does show up for you in the relationship. Appreciate it. Enjoy it. This acknowledgement and affirmation is not just meaningful for them, it's also reaffirming to you as to why you choose this relationship.

In all my years working with people, what I've found is that these long-term relationships hit the mark 80 percent of the time. Approximately 80 percent of expectations are met, and the non-negotiables are absolutely met. Sounds like a pretty healthy relationship, right? Even still, these relationships can begin to weaken or fail when we lose sight of the 80 percent and the fulfillment of our non-negotiable needs.

Instead, we may find ourselves obsessing about the one or two things the person is unwilling or incapable of doing. We are looking at one or a few of the components that make up only 20 percent of the relationship. Over time, we may not realize how damaging it is that 100 percent of our focus goes to the 20 percent that we are not pleased with. That's enough to burn the whole thing down. You are putting all of your attention on what you don't want.

This is why we name expectations and categorize them into needs, wants, and desires. Look at the things the other person is unwilling or incapable of showing up for in the relationship. Are they non-negotiable needs? If not, you're in great shape and need to redirect your focus to the 80 percent of your relationship that's really good. If they are not showing up for your non-negotiable needs, then it is on you to decide how to evolve the relationship.

You may have to accept that there are things in life that you love doing that the other person has no interest in. This may be in your relationships with your friends, your siblings, your children, or your romantic partners. For example, if you love bowling, go bowling. If the other person has no desire to roll a heavy ball down a lane to hit things, don't make it your mission to get them to bowl. Find someone else with whom you can go bowling.

This also applies to our professional relationships and the way we like to work. If you are a verbal processor and your business partner or staff member needs clear and concise communication, it is not your responsibility to make them enjoy and understand your daily verbal volcanic eruptions. Instead, find another professional with whom you can verbally process to get clear on your thoughts and then deliver those thoughts to your partner succinctly.

DON'T ASSUME THE PERSON WILL CHANGE

The third relationship saboteur is assuming the other person will change. This can be confusing to some, especially those who are new to my program and say things like, "Yeah, but aren't we changing ourselves so that the other person will change too?" The answer is no. We are changing ourselves to be the person who creates and nurtures relationships in a way that moves us toward our vision. The other person may or may not change. Either way, that's on them.

In a relationship, it's important to meet people where they are and not where you want them to be. If you find yourself looking to your boss, employee, friend, parent, child, or significant other to be different from who they've demonstrated they are, you will both suffer. They may never be able to live up to the avatar that you've created of them, and you will find yourself frustrated by them not being the person you created in your mind.

You may have had the experience of dating someone and developing the laundry list of little things you wish they'd change, believing it would make them perfect for you. Your mind might wander down the path of, "If I could just get him to shave a little more, a new wardrobe, maybe tune up the macros and get him to the gym…he'd be perfect." If you're approaching a person like a sculptor approaches a slab of stone, you're headed for trouble. They are not a raw material for you to shape in any way you desire.

I know a lot of people who communicate that children are not a thing they want to choose for themselves. Still, they find themselves opting in for children because of their parents' "need" for grandbabies. I see this happen all the time. Parents regularly pressure their adult children with statements like, "When are you going to have children?" or, "I'd really like to have grandkids!" or, "Your biological clock is ticking." Does anyone actually enjoy this type of coercion?

As obnoxious as it is, it does get some people to think, "Well, I never really wanted kids, but maybe I'm supposed to have them." They start to compromise their vision for their life to please the people around them. This is how people make the shift from having a relationship need for no kids to abandoning that need (or maybe it was just a want all along) and agreeing to bring children into the world. What they may not realize is that they were simply taking on someone else's need and making it their lifelong responsibility.

From the other perspective, if I know that I really want kids and I'm sitting across the table from somebody who's talking about the life they're creating and I'm not hearing cues about family, I'm going to just ask them directly, "Do you see yourself having a family one day?" If they say, "Nope," thank them for dinner and be on your merry way. Trying to force them to change or even just wishing they might someday are both recipes for disaster that will leave you feeling frustrated and unfulfilled. If you choose to pursue a relationship with them anyway, you're opting in with a person who was never going to meet that need for you.

Don't expect that the other person will change their mind. This is a terrible idea. A great way to mess up a relationship is to attempt to change the other person or assume (or even hope) they'll be different later. Does later for you mean a week from today? Two years? Oftentimes, we don't really think through the time frame we're expecting from our unrealistic ask, and then we get frustrated that our expectation is not being met in a way that feels timely enough.

If you find yourself thinking, "Everything is great, but..." you need to get very clear whether that "but" is a non-negotiable need, a want, or a desire. If it's a want or desire, give yourself permission to go without it. Stop looking to the same person to fulfill it. Get it fulfilled somewhere else. If it's a need, a non-negotiable, get out of there now, not later. Evolve the relationship. If someone is unwilling to show up for a need now, there is no evidence they're going to show up for it later. Don't wait for somebody to grow up, become more mature, or decide you're so wonderful, they'll change for you. Accept where they are. Don't live for potential change.

Your expectations, needs, wants, and desires will change over the course of a long-term relationship. What a human being wants or desires at twenty-five years old is vastly different than when they're in their forties. Since I was thirteen years old, I've been very clear that I'm not going to have kids. Family would say to me, "Joey, you're young. You'll change your mind." This lack of change over time is rare.

Despite my commitment to my decision, people didn't stop their attempts to change me and my needs. When I was seventeen, I got a similar response: "You're still young. I promise you're going to change your mind. You're absolutely going to want to have children." It came from all parts of my family–aunts, uncles, everybody.

By the time I was twenty-six, they tried a new approach to change me: acting concerned. Instead of telling me I'd change, they'd now ask, "What's wrong?" Essentially, my family thought there was something wrong with me because my desire for kids (or lack thereof) did not match theirs. They were worried because, according to them, having kids is what "everybody does." (Funny how that counters most advice we give teenagers to not do something just because everyone else is doing it!)

What's even more interesting, though, are the people who come up to me as an adult now and are fascinated by my ability to stick to my relationship needs. I vividly recall a close friend whispering, "Joey, how did you do it? Don't get me wrong, I love my family. I love my kids. But, how did you manage to not have kids?"

People's attempts to change us may be a constant occurrence in our lives. Unfortunately, many people aren't clear on their vision and thus abandon their own needs, wants, and desires for a story someone else sold them about how life is supposed to be. The way to avoid being changed by others in a way that isn't aligned with your vision isn't rocket science. Like me, you have to be mindful and intentional about what you want to create.

You've heard the old adage: "When we assume, we make an ass out of 'u' and 'me.'" This silly saying couldn't be more true. If you make assumptions that someone else will change, you're setting yourself up for failure. The same is true if someone makes this assumption of you. Be mindful of the times when assumptions are creeping into your relationships, because they're often a slow and painful road to relationship sabotage.

Assumptions also come into play in our communication. If you make assumptions about what the other person is feeling, thinking, or trying to say, you are incapable of receiving their communication. Why? Because you're not relating to them, you're relating to your assumption about them. Likewise, if you make assumptions about how they're going to respond to your communication, you are incapable of communicating effectively. When you go into the communication with a preconceived notion of how someone else is going to respond, you've limited what's possible in this conversation and in the relationship.

Take a moment and think about a time when you assumed something about someone. Think through how that conversation went. Think through how your assumptions influenced how you showed up for the conversation. When we assume what's going on for the other person, we make decisions based on that assumption rather than reality. It is true that people have varying degrees of self-awareness, and they may not be present with where they actually are emotionally. Nonetheless, when we base our approach on assumptions, it never goes well. The best rule of thumb is to take what someone says at face value and respond to what they communicate.

Instead, Accept What Is Happening

Acceptance is a challenging point for some people to understand. In our everyday language, acceptance may come across as permission for actions or behaviors that we are not okay with. Erase that definition from your mind for the purpose of this book and creating vibrant relationships. Acceptance is neither an agreement nor an endorsement of what's happening.

Instead, I want you to view acceptance as simply an acknowledgement of what's happening. Choose to accept where the other person is. This strategy replaces expecting people to change. You may not agree with what is happening or with what others do. You may not like where they are. You can choose to acknowledge that the person is behaving poorly, missing the mark, or making mistakes without expecting something different.

Acceptance during these times allows us to hold peace and compassion within ourselves. Holding this space with someone makes something better possible for them and creates opportunity. What people don't always realize is that when we accept people where they are, it gives us the clarity to respond accordingly. We're acknowledging the truth rather than looking at potential. Acceptance gives us access to developing extraordinary discernment to make choices in the relationship so that we stay aligned with our vision.

In the next section of the book, we'll get into what we need to recognize about the other person when it comes to creating our most vibrant and satisfying relationship experiences.

PART 3
THE OTHER PERSON

CHAPTER 9
KNOW THE OTHER PERSON

IT TAKES TWO TO TANGO.

Even though this section is about the other person in the relationship, I hope you have come to realize at this point that the relationship and what you want out of it will always come back to you. In this section, we'll be talking about the other person and their expectations, their own challenges and state, and how they show up for your vision. We will not be talking about how to coerce them into being the person you desire them to be. Remember, when it comes to relationships you are responsible for how you show up, and that's it. How you show up will, inevitably, have an influence on them. However, they always have the autonomy to decide how they respond. It's then up to you to decide what you want to do with that response.

This final section of the book revisits many of the concepts that you have learned about for yourself but from the perspective of the other person in the relationship. The other person may have a vision for their life and what they want their relationship with you to be. The other person most likely has expectations in the relationship and their own needs, wants, and desires. They have their non-negotiables and their way of communicating them (whether they do that effectively or not). Most importantly, they have their own emotional state that they are solely responsible for choosing or changing.

REVISITING ACCEPTANCE

Chances are you picked up this book or had it recommended to you because your relationship with another person is not what you hoped it would be. You are looking for the relationship to improve, and prior to reading the first two sections of this book, you probably hoped it would improve by the other person changing. Perhaps they had behaviors you found obnoxious or irritating. Perhaps you've opted in for years to a habit they have that has never been okay with you. Have you accepted that they're allowed to do what they choose to do for themselves?

Remember, when we talk about acceptance here, it's not in the traditional sense that we use the word; it doesn't mean you approve of or condone their behavior. Acceptance is simply the acknowledgment of what they're doing, acknowledgment of where they are and allowing it to be okay for them. Whatever someone is doing, is okay for them to do. If you don't accept that what someone is doing is okay for themselves, you'll be frustrated to no end. You can't change it.

The other person can only change it if they see value in changing and choose to develop a different capacity. If you expect them to be a certain way and they're not, you are choosing your own suffering. Otherwise, the only way for you to be happy is if they show up and do what you want, when you want it. That's a moving target, and it will never work.

Client Case Study Revisited: Owning Your State

Do you remember the story of Samantha and Jeff you read about in chapter 2? Samantha was disgusted with her husband Jeff's behavior and how he let his health go. While she didn't need him to look like he had in his twenties, she was concerned that the path he was on would lead to more severe health problems in the future. Plus, she no longer found him physically desirable due to his personal neglect. Samantha found herself maintaining this energy of disgust as she went about her day, and her daughters could pick up on the fact that she was feeling disgusted with their dad.

I reminded her that it was okay for Jeff to choose that for himself. I also remind her that she has opted in for this behavior for years now, which in essence was like condoning it because she didn't object to it. In order to move forward, she would have to accept and take ownership for the way the relationship was. It was a hard truth to hear, but Samantha realized that she couldn't force Jeff to change and instead had to change herself.

First, Samantha had to choose a state that she wanted to feel and bring that to the relationship. She chose compassion and worked to stay in the energy of compassion with her husband and around her daughters. Samantha also identified a strong "why" for wanting to maintain this expansive emotional state. She said, "I feel like I'm setting a terrible example for our daughters by tolerating behavior that isn't okay with me and then staying in this dysfunctional relationship where I feel disgusted most of the time. Our girls deserve better from both of us!"

Samantha identified that Jeff taking care of his health was a non-negotiable need for her. She communicated that to Jeff from a state of compassion, sharing that she loved him and wanted them to be active together like they used to and live as healthy as they could for as long as they could into the future. She asked if he would be willing to commit to working on his eating habits and would join her for a walk after dinner twice a week. Samantha committed to owning her state and being all in with Jeff for the next three months.

Initially, Jeff was taken aback by the request, partially because he had no idea that she had any desire to spend any time with him. She had been in a state of disgust for so long, he too had checked out of the relationship. At the same time, he had almost no desire to exercise and bristled at the thought of eating the "bunny food" (salads) that she occasionally ate for meals.

Samantha was excited that initially Jeff was joining her for after-dinner walks, though she began to grow frustrated when he would come up with excuses why he couldn't join her. Instead of falling back into her old pattern of disgust, though, she remembered to be all in on holding the energy of compassion while also communicating her needs. At the end of the three months, Jeff wasn't where she hoped he would be in his health, but she did note that he had made meaningful progress. He was now requesting additional walks together beyond the twice-weekly commitment, and she noticed that he had started to cut back on his soda habit and was drinking more water. Samantha found that this time together allowed them to talk more, in a way that they hadn't in their relationship for years. She communicated with him that she noticed the incremental changes he was making and how that made her feel toward him.

She decided to continue being all in for their relationship with an extended timeline to see what additional progress Jeff might make if she continued to show up with compassion rather than disgust. I got a letter from her about a year later that included a photo of her, Jeff, and their daughters after they had run a 5k together. She said that eventually something shifted in Jeff and he realized that he wanted to do better for her and for their daughters. The whole family grew closer because of it.

EXPRESSING VULNERABILITY

Vulnerability can be a tough topic. Some people express concerns about the vulnerability required sharing their needs, wants, and desires. In the previous case, Samantha felt a degree of vulnerability in finally communicating her needs. Jeff had his own degree of vulnerability in acknowledging where their relationship was and where he wanted it to be.

Sometimes people avoid vulnerability because they think it triggers feelings of insecurity or anger in them. They mistake the *discomfort* of being vulnerable for one of these fear-based emotions. The truth is that when we are feeling vulnerable, we are essentially in a love-based state.

Surprised? Think about it this way: When we are vulnerable, we are sharing something that matters to us with another person. We often do this because we are looking to improve our connection with each other. Vulnerability is only truly accessible from a love-based state. This is because a love-based state is the only space where we can love and be loved, and in that space we can offer the expression of vulnerability. You can't choose vulnerability in a fear-based state.

If expressing vulnerability with another person is love-based, why is it such a challenge? What sometimes happens is that vulnerability can become a trigger and something we're afraid of. This can happen when we've incorrectly linked pain to vulnerability at some point in our lives. Perhaps we experienced some pain in the past, but rather than tying the fear to the thing that happened we instead make vulnerability the culprit. We make the mistake thinking it was vulnerability that caused the pain.

An example of this is an affair in a monogamous relationship. Let's say you're in a monogamous relationship with someone, and they betray that trust by having an affair. You have been vulnerable with this person in many ways, as that is the nature of nearly all romantic relationships. It may feel like that vulnerability is the reason your partner's betrayal hurts so much. But your vulnerability is not the cause of your pain. Your pain is your response to your partner's disregard of an agreed-upon boundary. Opting in with someone who is not trustworthy has also caused the pain, not vulnerability.

People in these situations may enter future relationships with an energetic "wall" to protect themselves from the pain that they perceived came from vulnerability. Rather than assessing whether the other person is aligned with their vision and is trustworthy, they instead close themselves off from real connection, assuming that if the relationship ends it won't hurt as much as the last one. In this energetic state, they are setting up the next relationship to fail.

Vulnerability is what gives us access to love, connection, freedom, and all the wonderful things that we want to know in a relationship. In the future, we can check in with the people we are getting to know and make sure they have the capacity to meet the needs we have that are aligned with our vision. Once they demonstrate that capacity, we can let ourselves be open and vulnerable.

OWNING YOUR STATE AND THE OTHER PERSON

The expression "it takes two to tango" is true of any relationship—both parties must be engaged and willing to move together in order to make things work. Think about what you are in control of if you're dancing the tango with another person. You can control the way you move. You can control your timing, your facial expressions, and the energy you bring to the dance. The other person can probably pick up on whether you actually want to dance with them or not based on these things. You cannot control how they move, when they move, or how they feel about moving with you. Instead, you do your best to create space for them to be able to show up.

This analogy of a dance applies to how we need to think about our emotional state when we show up for any relationship. Just as you can't have a great dance with someone if you're in a state that feels like you're not ready to dance (exhausted, annoyed, insecure, angry, and so on), you can't set healthy expectations for your relationship if you don't manage yourself first. In a relationship, if your needs come from a place of insecurity, you're asking somebody to show up based on what you *don't* want. If you're feeling anger or resentment, or if you're caught in a sense of betrayal, your request of the other person is not going to be ideal. It's not going to work.

When we talk about changing the other person, we must return to our evaluation of our own state. We cannot change the other person, but we can influence how they show up based on how *we* show up. As you go through this section and think about the other person and what they do in your relationship, pay attention to what emotions come up for you. Take note of your ability to identify and manage your emotional state even as you're thinking about the other person and how the lessons in this book apply to them.

If you're in a fear-based state, you should not ask for the other person to meet your needs. It's most likely not a healthy ask. Even if the other person shows up and fulfills the ask, chances are you won't even be able to recognize it. Their response will not create the thing you're actually looking for if you're coming from a fear-based state.

These same principles apply to the other person. If they are in a fear-based state and try to express their needs to you, even if you attempt to show up and fulfill that need, it may not be enough for them. Have you had this happen in a relationship before?

While this often shows up in romantic relationships, it can play out in many other relationships as well. It may be the parent that is perpetually dissatisfied with you regardless of how much you try to show up for their needs. It may be the friend who feels insecure and requests that you spend more time together, but no amount of time seems to be enough for them. It's the boss who isn't meeting his numbers for the quarter and puts undue pressure on you, regardless of how you're delivering. A fear-based state will never provide anyone what they truly seek from the relationship.

You Are Not Responsible for Their Feelings

I've discussed how we cannot expect another person to make us feel happy, secure, fulfilled. You are responsible for your own emotional state. That applies to the other person as well. Although you influence each other, you are not responsible for how the other person feels.

I've heard it before. "But Joey, what if the other person in our relationship doesn't realize or accept that? What if they're not reading this book and they keep blaming me for the way they feel?" It doesn't matter what they say to you or how they try to blame you for their feelings; you know the truth about how emotional states work. You can try to share this knowledge with them (or tell them to get their own copy of this book), but recognize that they may not be open to it.

It's important to differentiate that we can do things to support the other person, but we cannot make ourselves responsible for them. If we find ourselves taking responsibility for their feelings, or if they try to convince us that we are responsible for how they feel, then we know a line has been crossed.

There is a fine and subtle line between supporting somebody when they're open to support and trying to control them to make yourself feel better. Supporting someone who is open to it benefits both people. Trying to control them to make ourselves feel better will only (temporarily) benefit us. Controlling another person is not healthy and will never move you toward your vision of the relationship. The same is true if the other person is attempting to control you.

Managing Your State in Conversations

Regardless of the other person's emotional state, you must be aware of and take control of yours. For example, let's say you want to engage in a conversation with your dad about him being upset. You plan on asking him if he's upset. Before you ask a single question to your dad, you need to check in with yourself first. What are you feeling when you make your inquiry? What's the emotion that's present for you as you think of having this conversation? Is it love and compassion? Fear? Anger? Be mindful when approaching conversations like these.

Take a moment to check in with yourself beforehand to ensure you are making the request from a place of love and compassion and not a place of fear. Ask yourself if you are looking to this person to manage your emotional state. If they are irritated, they most likely will not be able to help, because they are pissed off. The last thing you should do is ask an angry person to help you out with eliminating the fear you're feeling.

If you find that you're not in a state of love or compassion, the first step is to recognize what state you *are* in. This is called awareness. Chances are you are afraid, and that's not your dad's responsibility. He is upset. He is angry. Your dad is where he is. You can't do anything about that, especially if you yourself are afraid.

So, what *can* you do? Your first order of business is to do nothing, at least for right now. Your job is to manage your end of the relationship. Recognize that you're afraid or angry. Evaluate that feeling. Ask yourself, "If I engage with Dad from this place of fear, is it going to eliminate the fear? Is it going to create the outcome I desire, which is connection?"

The next step, called alignment, is what we need to do to get out of the fear and into a new love-based emotion. We do this by using the Four-Sided Breath. From a love-based emotion, we consider what action makes sense to move us toward the desired idea of connection. When the other person is angry, whether they are admitting it or masking it, consider if it is better to ask questions or leave them alone?

In those times when you're aware that you're not in an aligned state and you're not able or willing to align with a love-based emotion, disengagement is often the best course of action. If you decide not to disengage and instead try to push for a resolution before you are ready to own your emotional state, the most likely outcome is a fight. The best thing to do is to tend to your side first.

Managing Your State First

When we tend to our own state and shift into an expansive emotion, we often find that there are more courses of action available to us than we thought, and we often have greater clarity on the right action to take. This is important because the right thing in one moment may not be the right thing in the next. The right thing in one relationship may not be the right thing in another. Every situation is a little different.

Just because my significant other is upset, in one moment the right move might be to say, "Hey how are you? Is there something you'd like to share with me?" The next day or week, when they are upset again, the right move might be to give them space. No situation is exactly the same. Maybe they are a little bit open in one situation and obviously not in another. You're not going to be sensitive enough to see where they're at unless you manage your own emotional state first.

To tend to your end of the relationship:

1. Name the emotional state you are in.
2. Evaluate whether it is aligned with your vision for the relationship.
3. Align your state with your vision.
4. Take action from that space.

You will have a much greater understanding of what to do in your relationships when you get really good at these steps. I mean, really good! I can't emphasize this enough. Get really good at these steps and train your ability to shift your emotional state from a fear-based state to a love-based one. In a love-based state, you will know what to do. In a fear-based state, you'll fall right back into the safe ineffective patterns.

What I'm describing here is the use of your intuitive capacity. Intuition is a higher brain function, not the magical force it is often misunderstood to be. In Power of Intuition, we learn to leverage intuition to bridge the gap between where we are and where we want to be. Refer to the Resources section of this book for more information.

When you are in a state aligned with your vision, you can communicate your expectations and make requests of the other person. When they are in an aligned state, they are able to do the same. Understand that these requests, whether you are making them or receiving them, may come from a place of vulnerability. Acknowledge any emotions that may come up during this time, but keep yourself in an expansive emotional state and take action from that state. Watch how your relationship with the other person grows!

CHAPTER 10
EXPECTATIONS AND THE OTHER PERSON

NO ONE PERSON WILL MEET ALL OF YOUR EXPECTATIONS.

Let's start by revisiting the concept of relationship expectations. As mentioned in chapter 4, our expectations are the bar we set for ourselves, not how we will manage or change the other person. Expectations are our non-negotiable needs in the relationship, along with our wants and desires. We've talked about what we're asking the other person to show up for, how to communicate those expectations to them, and how to respond when our needs are met or unmet.

Now, we'll examine expectations from the perspective of the other person in the relationship. We'll look at what they need us to show up for and evaluate if those expectations are reasonable. We'll also discuss additional challenges with expectations, like when they are abstract and cannot be reasonably fulfilled, and how people can confuse their beliefs with their expectations.

THE OTHER PERSON'S NEEDS, WANTS, AND DESIRES

Have you considered what the other person's needs, wants, and desires might be within your relationship? Perhaps they've stated what they expect from you, though not using exactly the same terminology we use here. Perhaps they haven't explicitly stated their needs, wants, and desires but you have tried to infer what matters to them and what they expect from you in the relationship. In this section, we'll explore what it may look like when the other person shares their relationship expectations with you and the obstacles you may encounter with those requests.

When the other person shares an expectation for the relationship with you, it's important to evaluate if the expectation is reasonable and something that you can even consider showing up for. There are times in a relationship when a person feels like they're communicating their needs, wants, and desires effectively but these expectations aren't being met. There may be various reasons for this, including that the expectations are not reasonable, are abstract, or are actually beliefs.

UNREASONABLE EXPECTATIONS

Remember, our framework for evaluating whether an expectation is reasonable is as follows:

1. You clearly understand the expectation.

2. You are willing to fulfill the expectation.

3. You are capable of fulfilling the expectation.

4. The expectation aligns with the person's vision for your relationship.

When the other person is communicating their needs to you, it is helpful to make sure that you're on the same page with what is considered a need. As we've discussed, needs are the non-negotiables that allow you to continue the relationship. Wants are the things that are important to us but are not deal-breakers if they don't happen. Desires are like the cherry on top of the relationship—if they happen, it's great. They're things we enjoy or would make us feel good in the relationship, but their absence does not create painful feelings. Get clear with the other person on their expectations of you.

All that said, there are times when the other person may set an expectation and it's hard to hear because it's not a reasonable request. In contrast to reasonable expectations, the following framework can be used to define an unreasonable one:

1. The other person cannot communicate the expectation clearly and specifically; you don't clearly understand the expectation.

2. You are unwilling to fulfill the expectation.

3. You are incapable of fulfilling the expectation.

4. The expectation does not align you with the other person's vision for your relationship. (Remember, this relationship is a two-way street. You want the other person to show up in a way that aligns with your vision…and they want you to show up in a way that aligns with theirs.)

If any one of these criteria is at play, the expectation is unreasonable. No matter who is the source of the unreasonable expectation, there are three ways we can move forward: we can drop the expectation, evolve the expectation, or evolve the relationship.

Drop the Expectation

If an expectation isn't reasonable, the person holding it has the choice to drop it, to just let it go. This may sound like, "I just don't need to have this expectation met." Upon reflection, you or the other person may realize that what you were asking wasn't as necessary as it first felt. We cannot be expected or expect other people to be mind readers. If you've ever said or heard the words, "You should have known!" chances are there was an unreasonable expectation at play because a need was not clearly communicated. If an expectation is unreasonable, it may be worth dropping altogether.

Evolve the Expectation

An expectation might need to evolve if the person requesting the expectation is unable to communicate effectively in that moment. If you cannot clearly name your expectation for yourself, you need to evolve it. If the other person cannot clearly communicate their expectation in a way that you can understand, they are going to need to revisit what they want in a clear and specific way.

Evolving doesn't necessarily mean you need to change the expectation. It may need to be expressed differently, or it may need to get met somewhere else. For example, if I have been holding an expectation that my friend will go skiing with me but my friend hates skiing, I can ski with a different friend. Likewise, if a friend is requesting something from you that is not aligned with what you want from the relationship or life, explore if they can get their need met elsewhere. Not all expectations need to be met in any given relationship.

Evolve the Relationship

There are times when an expectation may result in the need to evolve the relationship. While ending relationships completely is not a common occurrence with the people who attend my intensives, there are occasions when the relationship is incompatible with one of the participant's visions.

One unrealistic expectation I've come across multiple times relates to monogamy. I'll have a married couple that enters into the relationship with the need for monogamy. The other person may decide they need to explore their sexuality with other people, in which case the marriage usually evolves and ends. I have seen people, though, who try to set a new (and often unreasonable) expectation by asking their partner to drop their need for monogamy and open up the relationship. I've heard things like, "I really love you, and I also love this person I've been having an affair with. Can't we make it work?" People try to set unreasonable expectations of the other person instead of recognizing that the relationship is at a point where it must evolve.

Evolving the relationship could mean the relationship transitions into a different type of relationship. Perhaps you are no longer romantic partners, but you become friends. Evolving may also look like cutting off contact with the other person completely. The point is, the relationship evolves so that one person is no longer attempting to meet the expectation they can't meet. You may need to communicate new expectations that you have of the newly defined relationship.

ABSTRACT EXPECTATIONS

Both parties in a relationship should also be aware of when the expectations being set are abstract. This happens when the person communicating the expectations is not clear with themselves on what they need or want. For example, saying something like, "I expect you to respect me" is an abstract expectation. It is unclear what "respect" means to the other person. Other common abstract expectations include statements like, "I expect you to be more affectionate," or, "I expect you to help out with the kids."

A person cannot fill an abstract expectation. Sometimes an abstract expectation is actually a clandestine attempt to get them to tend your side of the relationship. You may be looking to them to help you feel better about something. You may discover that what you thought was clearly defined is really not clear at all. If it's not clearly defined, it will never align you with your vision.

I have heard people say that they need the people they're in relationships with to be trustworthy. I understand where they're coming from, but I challenge them with this question, "Is the other person being trustworthy going to give you access to connection, peace, or joy in your vision?" The answer is no. It can't. The concept of "trustworthiness" means one thing to you, but it may mean something completely different to the other person. Trustworthiness to one person might mean only speaking the truth or not sharing anything that is untrue. To another person, being trustworthy means being transparent about what they do. Yet another person could see being trustworthy as keeping secrets well and not sharing private information that shouldn't be shared outside of the relationship.

If in my relationship I just agreed to be "trustworthy" without getting clarification of how that looks for you, we may both be puzzled when there is a disagreement or argument about whether or not I have been trustworthy. You expressed your need, I thought I was meeting your need, and we still ended up in a fight because the expectation was too abstract.

Another common abstract expectation is around being kind. If you asked five people in a room what kindness means to them, you would get five different answers. The mistake we make is that we believe we all have the same definition of these abstract concepts. We assume we have all agreed to the same "rules." Therefore, if someone in the relationship has a need for "kindness" but doesn't share exactly what that means or looks like to them, they are setting up the other person to fail.

Abstract expectations are not a good idea. An expectation needs to be clarified so the other person knows how you're expecting them to show up. In addition to those we've discussed, there are two abstract expectations that come up often and deserve some additional attention: love and tone of voice.

Expectations of Love

Let's look at the following script to explore how problematic abstract expectations of love can be.

Jane: "I need to know you love me."

John: "But, I do! I already friggin' do! What is it you need from me to feel that?"

Jane: "I need to feel loved."

Have you heard this conversation before? Perhaps you've even been on the giving or receiving end of it? Let's see how much you've learned so far. What is the problem with the apparent need that Jane is expressing?

If you answered that her request was abstract, you're right. And if you also answered that she was making John responsible for her feelings, then you've *really* been paying attention! It is inherently not possible for John to make Jane "feel loved." In relationships, you can love the other person, but it is their job to accept the love. Jane must take ownership of her feelings and emotional state.

At the same time, Jane could improve the quality of this conversation by being clear and specific with her expectations. Love, to her, might come from receiving gifts. Love might come in the form of quality time, and if that is so she needs to articulate what types of activities feel like quality time to her. For example, "I would like to go on weekend bike rides together like we used to in the early years of our relationship."

Love may also be expressed more specifically as words of affection and acknowledgement. Some people feel loved when they are thanked for doing work that might otherwise go unnoticed or unrecognized. Other people feel loved through touch and physical affection. Still others might feel loved the most through acts of service, such as doing the laundry, painting the living room, or servicing the cars. Express to your partner the way you'd like them to express love to you. If you're making the request because it affirms or it activates the way you already feel, you're good to go. If you're asking them to make you feel loved, though, you're setting both of you up for frustration and failure.

Expectations of Tone of Voice

I once had a session with a teenager and her father. At some point in the discussion, the father was getting more and more frustrated but was still talking in what I perceived to be a normal tone. (Though my perception of a "normal" tone may be slightly skewed by my own family upbringing). The teen said, "Don't yell at me!" and the father responded, "I'm not yelling at you. I'm speaking with passion." The teen responded with, "I feel like you're yelling at me," to which the father responded, "THIS IS YELLING!" as he lost it.

Is "not yelling" a reasonable or unreasonable request? The answer is not reasonable. What *is* yelling exactly? Oftentimes, if someone's asking somebody to not yell at them, they're actually looking to feel safe. They're trying to get the other person to behave in different ways so they feel better. The response is often, "I'm not yelling." This is not going to change how the person feels about their level of safety. In this situation, the father not yelling wouldn't actually be the thing that made the teen feel safe.

I reminded the teenager that she could not control her father's emotions or ask him to feel a different emotional way than how he was feeling. "Don't be angry around me," would not address what was really the need in the relationship. I told her, "It's not your job to control his end of the relationship. Be mindful of that." Then I encouraged her to look for a more specific way to define and communicate her needs to her father.

It's okay if somebody is angry at times when they're with you. You need to name the thing that's actually happening when they're upset. What's the action that they are taking that you would like to stop. What is it they're expressing when they get upset and when you perceive they're yelling? What are they expressing?

If you are in a situation with someone who you perceive to be yelling at you, do the following: Pretend there was no perceived increase in volume and you were to write the words down on paper. Are the words that the other person is communicating problematic for you? As an example, they might be blaming you. You can then set a more effective expectation, requesting that they not blame you for the things that are happening in the relationship. "I'd like to make the request that you don't blame me." That could be a reasonable and clear expectation. Blame is not a necessary part of communication, and the person should be able to communicate what they need to say without blaming. Plus, blame never moves anyone closer to their vision.

ARE EXPECTATIONS THE SAME AS BELIEFS?

One area that I find causes confusion is when people assume that their beliefs are expectations. That is not necessarily true. Just because I have a belief about something doesn't mean it's an expectation for how I need other people to show up. This gets confusing because oftentimes our expectations have been formed through our beliefs and value system, but our beliefs are not expectations themselves.

Both expectations and beliefs are tied to emotion. Both are a trigger for emotion.

We can illustrate this around the topic of sex. Someone may have a belief about sex, which may also show up as an expectation for them. For example, someone might hold the belief that if sex is requested of them, they have to perform. Or, if they have a belief that sex is dirty, that's not an expectation, but it's going to inform their expectations. They need to change the belief that sex is dirty if they're going to manage their expectations and have a healthy sexual relationship. Shifting their emotions and beliefs may inform those expectations.

In Power of Focus, we work with beliefs more in depth. Refer to the Resources section of this book for more information.

CHAPTER 11
EXPECTATION CHALLENGES

EXPECTATIONS ARE THE ROOT OF ALL SUFFERING.

A large part of this book has covered the expectations we have for the other person and the expectations they have for us. Expectations are one of the most important interplays of the relationship—identifying what our expectations are and who can meet them, communicating how we want or need our expectations to be met, and following through to make sure that what was communicated is fulfilled.

There are times, however, when our expectations may also cause us pain or struggle. There are times when our expectations may not come from a healthy place. And there are times when people will let us down. Let's explore some of the nuances that may arise from creating and fulfilling expectations.

MEETING NEEDS OVER TIME

As we experience life and enter different chapters in our lives, our expectations evolve. It's beneficial to check in with yourself, especially when entering into a new experience in your life. Ask yourself, "What are my current expectations? What are my needs? Have they changed? What are my wants?"

Conversely, understand that the other person is experiencing this same evolution. Their expectations for the relationship may also change with time, and you could find yourself caught off guard at the expression of new needs, wants, or desires. Maintaining strong communication and boundaries, while regularly assessing your needs, wants, and desires against your vision, is important to keep you aligned.

Let's say you're moving into a new phase of life in which you and your partner are retiring from the workforce. Your whole existence just evolved. Now, certain needs that were getting met may no longer be getting met. Work fulfilled a certain need for you that you may not even have identified. The need to be valued in a certain way may no longer be met through the career. Both parties retire and don't realize that their needs are not getting fulfilled anymore.

When this happens, it's not uncommon for individuals to blame the other person. They might say things like, "What did you do to me? We were fine until I lived with you all the time." Actually, it had nothing to do with your partner. They're doing exactly the same thing they have always done with you. The difference is that you had a need that your work fulfilled for you in a way that the other person cannot (or that you cannot fulfill for them).

In these situations, your expectations of the relationship need to be reevaluated. If you have a need to feel productive and like a contributor, it is your responsibility to find other avenues that might meet this need. Perhaps you can volunteer or find a part-time, low-stress job. Maybe it's time to pick up that hobby you've always wanted to try.

If you or the other person in your relationship find that your life has evolved and you now have a need that is going unmet, follow this framework:

1. Identify the need that is not being met and name it.

2. Ask yourself, "How am I going to get this need met?"

3. Select the method that aligns with your vision and meets your needs.

That simple second question can be a game changer. You just have to remember to ask it.

MANIPULATION VERSUS INFLUENCE

When we or the other person are looking to get needs met, it's important to understand if this is being done through manipulation or influence. Manipulation is what occurs when a person attempts to get their needs met by any means necessary without regard for the other person. It is a focus on the person with the need using tactics to get what they want because they want it. Manipulation disregards the other person and their best interests entirely. It is not a healthy or positive way to conduct a relationship.

Meanwhile, influence is a focus on the other person and what is in their highest and best interest. The person with the need may also benefit from the outcome of this influence, but it is born of selflessness. Getting needs met from a place of influence is in service and support to the other person and their benefit.

We influence others when we work from an expansive emotional state. We show up better and, in turn, the other person gets the best version of us and has the opportunity to show up better as well. When we show up in the world in a selfless way and aim to leverage influence in our relationships to the benefit of the people in our lives, we tend to receive so much more as a result.

RELY ON WHAT PEOPLE DO, NOT WHAT THEY SAY

Don't rely on what people say. Trust what people do. People communicate mostly in two ways: verbally and through action. Over the years, I've heard so many people promise me they are going to do things. They are adamant that they'll follow through. I have learned to maintain no expectation that they're actually going to do so.

I've realized it's just a numbers thing. If 1,000 people tell me they're going to do something, one in 1,000 will actually execute on what they say they will do. I don't pay attention to the things people say; I watch what they do. I make my decisions on how I'm going to relate to somebody based on what I see them do, way more than on what they say.

For example, in working with colleagues I pay attention to the regularity of their follow-through. This helps me know in future situations who I can reasonably expect to do what they say they'll do and who might be all talk. Why does that matter? Because without this knowledge, I am setting myself up to be let down.

Expectations are the root of all suffering. If you notice you feel pain, if you stop and have the wherewithal to ask yourself what expectation isn't being met, chances are you will be able to discover an expectation that you thought would be met but wasn't. You are still allowed to hold that expectation, but you need to acknowledge that the other person is unlikely to meet it.

Most people blame other people for their own suffering. If someone asks, "What do I do about someone who lies to me? Can I have the expectation that they don't lie?" I ask them if the other person frequently lies. If the other person is a frequent liar, then asking them not to lie is not a reasonable expectation. You are creating an expectation for them to do something that they might not be capable of doing. In these situations, we need to evolve our expectations or evolve the relationship. Otherwise, you are the cause of your own suffering. It's way easier to evolve your expectation than to evolve the other person.

CLOSING THE LOOP

Have you ever been in a relationship in which things are going really well and you're feeling great, then all of a sudden it's not so great. We wonder what happened and why things changed. The reason is often because you didn't know what expectations were present in the relationship. If that's the case, it's time to reflect on what your expectations are and have a conversation with the other person in the relationship to understand their expectations as well.

It always starts by naming the expectation so you can ensure that you keep showing up for it for yourself and for the other person. Knowing your expectations and communicating them enables the other person to keep showing up for you, and you can show up for them, promoting a thriving and vibrant relationship. This is what I refer to as closing the loop.

Once we've named the expectation clearly for ourselves, we close the loop by having the conversation. We need to get to the place where we accept the relationship for where it is, meaning accepting that the expectation is clear and whether the person is willing or unwilling to show up for it.

If the other person accepts the expectation and is willing to show up for it, what does that mean? It means you can count on them to show up for it, and that will be wonderful. You both will have a great time doing that together.

The other person also has the option to opt out. In this case, check in again with yourself and make sure that what you're expecting of them is not a non-negotiable need. The other person can opt out of your wants or desires without you having to evolve the relationship. If you accept they're not willing to show up for your request, then moving forward you're not going to look for them to show up for that expectation.

Let's return to the example of skiing. You love to ski and you want to enjoy that experience with people in your life. You may hope that your friend will fulfill this need for you. If you ask them to ski with you and they say "no", it's important to understand that it may not be a "no" forever and could just be a "not today" or "not this year." Perhaps the next time you invite them it will be a "yes."

For you to feel best in the relationship, it's important that you not hold an expectation that your friend will fulfill this for you. In keeping yourself open, you give yourself the ability to have the need met elsewhere. This is why we have lots of different kinds of relationships. This is why we have community. Your significant other is not supposed to be all things for you. Your friend is not supposed to be all things for you. No human being is supposed to be all things for you. And you're not anybody's everything either. Nor should you ever try to be.

When you feel hurt, there's emotional pain there. You may feel sad, unworthy, angry, or resentful. Ask yourself, "What expectation did I have? Even if I was not aware I was holding an expectation, what expectation did I have that did not get met?" Pay attention to the story you tell yourself in those moments. I often hear people use stories like, "They don't love me," "they don't understand me," or "they don't respect me" in cases like these.

Instead of going into that theme of blame, making the other person responsible for where you are, ask yourself what expectation did not get met. Name the expectation, so you can take steps to evaluate it. Was it reasonable? Does it align with your vision? Did you communicate it clearly and specifically? Did the other person opt in? Were they capable?

On the other side of things, when you feel happy, fulfilled, joyful, or compassionate, ask yourself the question, "What expectation is getting met here?" If you want to make it really simple, name the expectations that are getting met, that light you up, and that are moving you toward the vision of what you want in the relationship. Get clear on what those expectations are. Communicate them to the other person with appreciation, and show up for each other in that consistently.

Knowing your expectations and communicating them enables the other person to keep showing up for you, and you can show up for them, promoting a thriving and vibrant relationship.

EMOTIONAL RESILIENCE

The goal of this chapter is to understand that there will be situations and circumstances in which our expectations aren't met. My hope for you is that you reach a place through consistent practice and training where you develop emotional resilience. Emotional resilience is the ability to maintain the emotion we choose even when the environment isn't fulfilling our expectations.

Think about the expansive emotions you identified at the beginning of this book. What are the emotions that seem most aligned with your vision for life and for your relationships? It is imperative that you train yourself to maintain these emotional states, regardless of how the other person is showing up for you. While it may feel like you're doing this training to benefit the other person, the truth is that you need emotional resilience to benefit you.

When you have become fluent in emotional resilience, you will be surprised by the shifts you may see in your life. People will respond differently to you, and you may have access to new opportunities and perspectives that you didn't in your previous emotional state. Be aware of the expectation pitfalls discussed in this chapter, but understand that you have control over how you show up. Choose emotional resilience, and you're choosing to align with vision.

CHAPTER 12
VISION AND THE OTHER PERSON

*FREEDOM LIES IN THE ABILITY TO
ACCEPT THE OTHER PERSON.*

Has the other person in your relationship read this book? Perhaps you received it from them so that you both can communicate and work together using the same education and tools. It may be that you're the first one to read this content and the other person does not yet have the same level of knowledge on how to approach your relationship for the most vibrant and fulfilling outcome.

In this final chapter, we'll recap our view of vision and how the other person may or may not show up for it. With this knowledge, you'll be able to move your relationship forward in a way that honors both your needs and the other person's capacity.

THE OTHER PERSON'S SIDE OF THE RELATIONSHIP

When we are doing the work to be in an expansive emotional state, it is not uncommon for the other person in the relationship to want to feel the same. Where they may miss the mark, though, is in assuming that you can help them manage their emotional state. If your person comes up to you, wanting you to help them manage their state, don't attempt to make them feel better. Remember the first story I told about my ex-girlfriend who wanted me to help her feel more secure? There were no words or actions I could say or do that could make her feel that. Don't allow another person to make you responsible for how they feel.

Start by reminding yourself, "I'm not going to make myself responsible for where they are." Revisit the rules of the relationship: there's my end of the relationship, there's the relationship itself, and there's the other person's end of the relationship. Recognize that this person is asking you to be responsible for how they feel. Set the boundary to not do that.

What can you do instead? Let's say, for example, that the other person is angry. They may admit that they're angry or they may not and mask it, but you can sense that they're in an emotional energy of anger. If you don't have access to any other tool, non-engagement may be your best option. If they're not in a good place to engage, you can go to another room or end the call to disengage for the time being. You are not responsible for how they feel, and they cannot make you responsible for it. Staying and trying to work through things when they are in a contracted emotional state will often result in a fight. The best thing to do is to tend our side first.

Disengagement is not our only option, though. The right thing to do in one moment may not be the best thing in the next. For example, if your significant other, sibling, or friend is upset, it may be a situation that should be addressed immediately. Depending on the circumstance, you may choose to check in and say, "Hey, how are you? Is there something you'd like to share with me?" The next week when you notice they are upset, the best move might be to give them space. No two situations are exactly the same. Anger may be present in two different situations. In one, the other person is open to sharing; in another, perhaps they are not. You are not going to be sensitive enough to discern where they are or to have an intuition of how to best respond unless you manage your space first. So, the first step is always to tend to your end of the relationship. Name it, evaluate it, align, and then take action.

If they're asking you to manage their emotions, you might say something like, "I clearly see that you're struggling. You're asking me for help. I'm not the person to help you with this. I don't know how. Here's something that could help." Invite them to read this book or attend an Inner Matrix program from the Resources section of this book. If you have a tool that can help your person, invite them to engage the tool. If they don't, that's okay. They are allowed to say no. Don't make yourself responsible for how they feel. If you stop and realize that this person is clearly asking you to be responsible for how they feel, be clear that you can't do that. Instead, center yourself and get to a place where you can influence.

What I find is that when we engage with clarity, having tended our side of the relationship, the other person has an opportunity to stop and think. Maybe they don't get what you're doing or saying to them at that moment. Maybe they get really pissed off because they don't like what they're hearing. Maybe they feel more hurt initially. More often than not, though, when they leave that conversation and have some time to think through things, they'll come to realize their part. They are less likely to come to the realization if you feed their insecurity.

ACKNOWLEDGE HOW THEY SHOW UP FOR THE VISION

We all want to be seen and acknowledged, yet it's so easy to be critical in our relationships. Biologically, we have a negative bias to focus on threats and ways to eliminate them. According to a recent research article from Swarthmore College on negative bias, "Negative information has stronger effects on attention, perception, memory, physiology, affect, behavior, motivation, and decision-making than does equally extreme and arousing positive information."[6] That negative bias is baked into us at an evolutionary level. That's great when it comes to basic human survival, but it adds an additional layer of complexity to forming and maintaining positive relationships.

It takes conscious focus and intention to see and appreciate all that is good in our relationship. In most of our relationships, 90 percent of it is probably great—supportive, uplifting, positive. Yet somehow we find ourselves obsessing about how our friend wasn't available when we needed them, how our business partner dropped the ball on that project, or how our partner parked badly in the garage. Don't even get me started on the dishwasher—dishwashers destroy relationships.

Develop the skill and routine of acknowledging the simple things you appreciate about the other person. Don't wait for them

---

[6] Catherine Norris. (2021). "The Negativity Bias, Revisited: Evidence From Neuroscience Measures And An Individual Differences Approach". *Social Neuroscience*. Volume 16, DOI: 10.1080/ 17470919.2019.1696225. https://works.swarthmore.edu/fac-psychology/1125.

to go first. You take that step in support of this relationship thriving. Acknowledge how they show up for the relationship vision—affirm and appreciate them. And name for them the impact it has on you when they show up in this way.

ACKNOWLEDGE HOW THEY DON'T SHOW UP FOR THE VISION

Likewise, we must not shy away from things that aren't working. Things left untended will not go away on their own. We all make mistakes. We all have bad days and challenging seasons. Things can start out as minor annoyances, but if we don't tend to them, they have a way of growing over time and becoming a big deal.

It's a lot easier to tend something when the intensity is low and it's not a big deal. When assessing what needs tending in your relationship, go back to your list of needs, wants, and desires. Definitely tend to needs, and do so sooner rather than later. Consider tending to your wants, particularly if they are important to you. If the miss is around a desire, it's probably best to let it go.

When you do address ways in which the other person isn't showing up for the vision, align yourself first, then communicate the expectation, the boundary that was missed, and the impact it had on you. When you manage your side of the relationship well and you stay in integrity with your end of vision, your feedback and your requests will be better received. You must be willing to name and tend to what's happening in your relationships in order for you to realize the vision you have for relationships and for life.

WHO IS RESPONSIBLE FOR WHAT?

The other person is responsible for their actions. You are responsible for the impact you experience. If you need the other person to do something different in order for you to feel better, you've given away your power, which sounds like, "They need to change in order for me to feel okay." This is in no way meant to excuse bad behavior. It is a way of owning your own space so you are able to set boundaries from an aligned state.

If you lose yourself because someone else is in a bad mood it will be very challenging to hold a space in your relationship to ensure that it thrives. You must endeavor to respond in alignment with your vision always! Even in circumstances where it would be totally reasonable to lash out or defend yourself, don't do it. Call yourself into alignment with your vision, and find a way to respond from that place.

This can look like setting a boundary and disengaging from an aligned state. Always go to vision first. Ask, "How can I show up for my vision for this relationship in this circumstance? This practice will change the game and make your vision a reality. Be uncompromising in your commitment to hold a space of love for people, compassion for yourself, and inspiration. Do this no matter what is said to you or what is happening around you. You deserve to live in an expansive energy.

MANAGING YOURSELF AND THE OTHER PERSON

Perhaps you entered this section on the other person hoping that some of the responsibility for the relationship was on their shoulders. Maybe you still had a piece inside of you that was looking for permission to blame them for the way things are. You won't find that here.

You are responsible for yourself and the way you feel. You can't manage yourself through the other person. Some people try to get the other person to do something, to try to manage their own internal pain, insecurity, or unworthiness. You also can't manage somebody else's pain, insecurity, or unworthiness. That's you trying to manage them. If you remember back to my first story of my ex-girlfriend who needed to feel secure, no matter what I did to try and manage her feelings, it only served to strain our relationship more.

If there's a struggle with someone, it's often tied to trying to manage that person in some way. It's exhausting and impossible. The aspect of the relationship that is not your responsibility is the other person. That's their responsibility. They're the only person who can do something about their emotions, their thoughts, their actions. You are responsible for you.

Ask yourself when you are most frustrated with the person you're working with. What do they say or do that is causing friction in your relationship? In turn, are you trying to manage something they do? Doesn't it drive you up the wall when they go against what you want them to do? Of course it does. But nothing you say or do can effectively control what they're going to do.

What you can do, however, is focus on how you respond to them. When you attempt to be responsible for the other person's end of the relationship, you are completely out of control. You simply cannot control other people. As a human, I forget this sometimes. A person will behave a certain way and I'll have a desire to try to change their behavior. When I forget how people work, things don't go well. It's in these moments of frustration that I remind myself to take a breath and step out of the situation. Having this space allows me to assess what went wrong, remember who is responsible for what, and get clear on what I can influence. It's in our realm of influence that we have our power.

When we do something solely for the other person, not so that we get something out of it for ourselves, we have the ability to influence the relationship. We are accepting the other person for who they are. When we try to control someone, we are signaling that we don't accept them.

If we're trying to determine who was right and who was wrong in the relationship, then we are not looking to accept the other person. As soon as you decide they're wrong, you're setting yourself up to be let down. When you can accept where the other person is, it gives you the ability to influence from a place of acceptance, which is a love-based state. I can't emphasize this enough. You can't influence another person until you accept them.

Pay attention to your own experiences with this. Can you think of a time when somebody was not in a place of acceptance with you and they had an agenda of what they thought you should do? What was your response? It's highly unlikely that you said, "Wow, thank you so much for that great, unsolicited advice. Let me go turn my life around!" Chances are it was a natural reaction for you to resist their attempt at controlling you. Most likely you did not have good feelings toward the person, and you probably were not in the emotional state to want to improve your relationship with them at that point. Control destroys relationships.

What part of the relationship can you control? Yourself and what you put into the relationship.

What can you not control? The other person and what they put into the relationship.

While this book discusses your role in the relationship, the relationship itself, and the other person, I hope you realize by now that this work all goes back to you. You are at the start of a journey that will fundamentally change the way you move through this world and relate to others. Regardless of the relationship you're in, the relationship will always go back to you and what you choose to put into it. Keep training and you will almost certainly have a vibrant future ahead!

CONCLUSION

CHAPTER 13
VIBRANT ROUTINES

INTENTIONS DON'T TRANSLATE TO NEW OUTCOMES. CONSISTENT, ALIGNED ACTION OVER TIME DOES.

Have you ever attended a speech, conference, or event where the message really resonated with you? Perhaps it even inspired you to change your life. You left fired up to move into this new way of living. You told the people closest to you how excited you were. You started the work to change…and then real life crept back in, and you found that your energy for that life change became an echo of the past.

It's not uncommon for people to intellectually understand a concept and agree with it but never actually integrate it into their lives. Why? There seem to be two primary reasons. The first relates to motivation to change. A research study by the Healthy Life Centres in Norway found that "lifestyle change is more likely to be initiated and maintained when goals are not only achievable but also regulated with autonomous motivation and of intrinsic value. Conversely, lifestyle change is difficult to maintain when motives are external to the self."[7]

This is why my approach to transforming relationships works for so many people: it all centers around you and what is of intrinsic value to you. Yes, the things and stuff that may result from these strengthened relationships are great, but the real benefit to you doing this work is the emotional state you now operate in. You are more likely to continue doing this work because you'll begin to see how good it feels to be in an expansive emotional state of joy, compassion, or love. When you feel it enough, you will not want to return to your previous states of anger, fear, or insecurity.

The other reason people don't always integrate a new way of being into their lives is because it never becomes a routine, and thus never turns into a consistent, automatic response. Think of it like walking. At some point in your life, you couldn't walk. As a toddler, you may have seen others walking and had the desire to pull yourself up in your crib or with the help of a coffee table.

Eventually, you were wobbling across the floor step by step. Every bit of your energy went into focusing on how to move yourself forward. With time and repeated practice, you reached the point where walking no longer felt like such an effort. Eventually, you reached the point where you could stand up and walk with little thought. Walking became an automatic response. Your body and mind knew how to do it without expending much energy to figure

---

7   Sevild, Cille H., et al. "Initiation and Maintenance of Lifestyle Changes among Participants in a Healthy Life Centre: A Qualitative Study." *BMC Public Health*, U.S. National Library of Medicine, 26 June 2020. pmc.ncbi.nlm.nih.gov/articles/PMC7318496/#Bib1.

out how. As long as you keep walking, your mind and body know what to do.

You can have a joyful and expansive relationship for years, decades even, but if you step out of your routines for too long, your relationships can wither once again. One way I think about people, including myself, is that we have an old habit self. But we all have the ability to cultivate a new habit self. It might be more accurate to say, we can create new routines. The mind can be a bit lazy. It takes very little effort to act from our old habit self. It takes much more intentional mental effort to cultivate new routines. The way we do this is by learning effective techniques and practice, practice, practice.

HABIT VERSUS ROUTINE

Habits and routines are a set of things we do over and over—they're both reflexes that occur automatically. For me, the difference between a habit and a routine is that a habit is an unconscious behavior we engage in, while a routine is intentionally designed and adopted in order to get a specific outcome.

For example, if you have a regular habit of biting your nails, would you say that you consciously choose to bite them because you like scraggly fingertips? Of course not. Nail-biting is an unconscious habit that may become a regular part of your life. The same can be said for people who are naysayers. I would hope that nobody consciously chooses to point out the downside in every situation on purpose, and yet for some people it seems to be an unconscious default with no specific desired outcome…unless they're trying to get invited to fewer social gatherings.

A routine is something we intentionally design and adopt in order to get an outcome. Checking in and naming our emotional state can become a routine. Engaging the Four-Sided Breath in stressful situations may become a routine. We have intentionally chosen to add these things to our lives because they are aligned with our vision for life.

Now that we have a vision for life, our actions should be aligned with that vision. This is what I refer to as creating vibrant routines. When you choose actions that are aligned with your vision and you repeat them often, you ensure that you will have fulfilling, vibrant relationships in every area of your life. That is something most people only dream of.

TRAIN NEW RELATIONSHIP PATTERNS

In any relationship you choose to work on going forward, it's important to return to the first step of identifying your vision. Sometimes it's easier to focus on the past. We fall into old habits of blaming the other person for what they've done and how it made us feel. It may be a challenge to start a fresh perspective of the relationship.

Focus on where you're going, starting right here, right now, rather than focusing on the past and what may have happened or gone wrong. Focus on the vision for the relationship and on the steps you can take right now to move in that direction. If you put your attention and focus there consistently, you're going to hit the mark.

Be Aware of What to Stop Doing

The first step in training new conscious routines in your relationship is to recognize what you need to stop doing. What are you currently doing that is breaking the relationship down and leading you away from your vision? Name one key thing that you're going to stop doing, like, "I'm going to stop criticizing my daughter," or, "I'm going to stop threatening to sell the business."

And the best way to stop doing something is to do something else.

Create and Execute a Training Plan

Just focusing on a new conscious routine will support you to stop doing the thing you need to stop. Name one thing (yes, just one) that you're going to start doing as a conscious routine consistently over time such as, "I'm going to start experiencing love and gratitude within myself and expressing it to my partner." If it's related to your business you might say, "I'm going to start affirming and acknowledging my team." Choose one routine that you are confident you have the ability to implement and then dedicate yourself to consistently making it a part of your day.

Be aware that your intentions alone won't translate to new outcomes. We can think all of the good things we want, but the truth is that nothing will change without action. Consistent, aligned action over time translates to new outcomes. Period.

If new outcomes are what you want, whether in your relationship, in your business, in the way you manage your finances, or whatever aspect of your life you're looking to change, you need to create and execute a training plan. This means deciding what actions you're going to take and then being rigorous in your commitment to follow through.

To improve your odds at having a successful outcome, I suggest executing just one new conscious routine at a time. Execute it every day until it becomes a reflex. Once it becomes a reflex, add another new conscious routine. It's the slow and steady approach that will lead to long-term mastery.

Confirm the New Reflex

The more you execute the new way of being, the faster it becomes a reflex. For example, if your one thing is to affirm others, you can affirm others a few times a week. It may take six months for it to become a reflex. If you affirm others twenty times a day, it may take a few weeks. When you notice that you're affirming people in your mind rather than criticizing them, you've developed the reflex. Now watch your life begin to shift!

CHAPTER 14
MY HOPE FOR YOU

Dear Reader,

We've reached the end of this book, but my hope is that this is not the end of our journey together. The truth is I didn't write this book for it to be a standalone source of information for you to improve your life. It is simply the starting point to open your mind to what your relationships and your life can be.

My motivation to enter the realm of personal development and transformational work was initially my desire to make families work in a healthier way. My own childhood was full of pain, fear, and sadness. When I realized something else was possible, a better way of being and relating to each other, I wanted to make it available to people. I didn't want another child to experience what I had gone through. I was able to pull myself out of it. Most aren't so lucky and end up repeating the cycle for generations.

But my work goes beyond family dynamics. Because relationships impact every aspect of our lives, from how we earn income, to how we feel safe, to how we find community, I realized that I wanted to share this knowledge of how to create expansive emotions within ourselves and cultivate strong, healthy relationships with others. I have seen that there is a better way to move through this world, and my hope is that you will get to experience it too.

I know what you may be thinking. I know it because I've worked with thousands of people who have reached this inflection point. There will be that voice in your mind that questions if this is actually possible. I hear it occasionally in my intensives when someone will say, "Well, maybe my relationship could be better, but I am not sure that it can, and I'm afraid to make a change." There's the fear that if they create a vision and communicate their expectations, it will dismantle the life they have and they'll be left with nothing. The fear of the unknown and the seductive draw of what is familiar to them is what keeps them stuck in relationships that are "good enough" but ultimately leave them feeling disappointed, disconnected, and empty.

They are correct in that if they follow the teachings of this book and my other trainings, they will dismantle the life they had. But instead of being left with nothing, they will be creating the life they've always wanted to live. It's like the tree that loses its leaves in the fall to create space for new, fresh, healthy leaves to grow in their place. The tree's life is not over in the fall, it's simply experiencing growth. Have the courage to let go, lean in, and go for change. Even having the courage to *believe* a better life is possible is part of the warrior's journey. I promise you that something better is waiting for you on the other side if you're willing to continue moving forward.

Are you willing to experience short-term discomfort in exchange for a lifetime of fulfillment and possibility? Or will you opt for short-term comfort in exchange for a lifetime of suffering and regret?

Do you continue this path forward, deepening your knowledge of self, tenaciously pursuing your vision for life, and repatterning old beliefs and emotions along the way? Will you continue to hold yourself accountable for establishing vibrant routines in your life? Will you have the hard conversations and set the boundaries you need to thrive in this life?

Or will you say, "That's nice," close this book, and quickly return to the patterns that brought you here in the first place? This is your time to decide. It's a pivot point in your life story. It's both exciting and frightening because it means going through the process of change. I know because I've been there many times. I can undoubtedly say that every step I have taken in my life that moved me toward my vision has brought me more joy and more satisfaction than I ever imagined.

My wish for you is that this book does not end up in the "Shelf Help" section of your home library. You deserve better, and you've got this life and this opportunity to do it now. Your emotional energy matters. Your relationships matter. Your quality of life matters.

You matter.

—JOEY KLEIN

ACKNOWLEDGEMENTS

To you, the reader: Thank you for your courage to grow and evolve in pursuit of creating stronger, more meaningful relationships. Your willingness to take action toward transformation inspires the heart of this book.

To my clients - past, present, and future: Your trust in allowing me to support you in reaching new outcomes in your relationships has been a gift. Your journeys have provided invaluable insights and have shaped the content of this work.

To my core mentors: Your insistence that I train others as part of my education has been a cornerstone of my growth and teaching. Your wisdom and vision continue to resonate through every page of this book and corner of my company.

To my amazing team of Trainers: Your passion, dedication, and focused efforts are priceless. It's a privilege to work alongside individuals so deeply committed to making a positive impact.

To my amazing Team: Each interaction with you deepens my gratitude. You bring excellence, compassion, and energy to everything we do together, and this book is better for it.

To Dr. Lydia Glass: Thank you for your foreword and for your dedication to the training. Your belief in the importance of this book has been a source of encouragement.

To Jillian Abby, my writing partner: Working with you has been a true joy. Although writing a book isn't high on my list of favorite things to do, you kept me on track and diligent. You also helped me to crystalize and clarify the key concepts that brought this book together. I'm deeply grateful for your contributions.

To Wendy Walcott: Thank you for your consistent loyalty and passion towards what we have set out to build; this book is in service to that vision.

To Kate Simmons: Thank you for your ability to "speak fluent Joey Klein" and for helping shape this book into something I'm incredibly proud of. Your clarity and understanding were instrumental.

To Caitlyn Fagan: Thank you for your ability to move balls down the field, no matter what, with relentless passion.

To all who have contributed, supported, and encouraged me along this journey, thank you. This book is a direct reflection of your grit and grace.

INNER MATRIX SYSTEMS MEMBERSHIP

Train the fundamentals with like-minded, growth-oriented high achievers through an Inner Matrix Systems Membership. A cornerstone of having vibrant relationships is developing our capacity to manage our side of the relationship, which includes managing ourselves emotionally and mentally.

Inner Matrix Systems offers a foundational curriculum, The Power Series, that trains people all over the world to develop and master themselves, and create lives better than they imagined possible.

Learn to still, focus, and direct the mind through Power of Focus. Master the art of mindset training, so the mind will no longer keep you from the relationships you could have.

Jump into Power of Emotion to develop your emotional intelligence and acuity. Master your emotions, and you'll master not only your relationships, but your life.

Develop the ability to name and create your vision through Power of Vision. Vision is a skill that isn't taught at home or at school. In order to create what you want, the first step is to name it.

Finally, if you are unsure of how to move forward and don't know what to focus on first, Power of Intuition will support you to develop and leverage the skill of intuition. Intuition bridges the gap between where you are and where you want to go.

Visit InnerMatrixSystems.com/Membership_Overview to learn more about Membership.

BETTER THAN BUSINESS SCHOOL

By invitation only, Elite Cohort is a year-round training curriculum that dives into the inner workings of what drives success and outcomes. Elite Cohort Members learn how to guarantee their desired outcomes in their fully fulfilled, inspired, and joyful lives.

THE FORMULA FOR GOING FURTHER, FASTER

This year-long cohort is designed to train you inside the deepest strategies of personal mastery, not only to supercharge your already epic results, but to ensure your life is one of fulfillment and purpose.

Core Training Topics

- Vision
- State Training
- Leadership
- Relationship Management
- Business & Career Advancement
- Investing
- Health Optimization
- Biohacking
- Principles & Purpose

Visit JoeyKlein.com/Work-With-Me to learn more about Elite Cohort.

1:1 MASTERY TRAINING

IT'S WHAT YOU WISH THERAPY WAS

By invitation only, and currently on a wait list, Joey limits his private practice to individuals who want to live all-out and make an impact with their lives. He supports high achievers to not only create epic outcomes, but to love the life they have worked so hard for.

THE TRAINING

In Joey's 1:1 Mastery Training, you're not just getting a trainer—you're getting a partner who is personally committed to achieving your desired outcome. Joey works tirelessly and uses his proven training formulas to provide the exact steps his clients need to turn their visions into reality—whatever they may be.

In Joey's Words

Everybody's got a coach—a life coach, an executive coach, a parenting coach, even a sex coach. I am not a coach. I'm not here to be your cheerleader, or simply share information, or tell you what to do. I am a Trainer—I partner with you to create the results you name for yourself.

Visit <u>JoeyKlein.com/Work-With-Me</u> to learn more about 1:1 Mastery Training.

SPEAKING

IGNITE TRANSFORMATION

Joey Klein doesn't just speak. He ignites transformation. Whether presenting a keynote to a 1,000-person audience or leading a 25-person virtual workshop, Joey brings his proven systems for personal mastery to your stage. These aren't just talks—they're catalysts for real, measurable change in your organization.

KEYNOTES, WORKSHOPS, CUSTOM TRAINING PROGRAMS

No Cookie-Cutter Talks

Joey knows that new results demand new actions. That's why he's never given the same presentation twice. Instead, he tailors each talk to the needs and desired outcomes of his audience to ensure real results.

Podcasts & Media

Joey's unique perspective on personal mastery and his varied background in meditation, martial arts, psychology, and neuroscience make for compelling conversations that resonate with audiences seeking growth and transformation.

Visit JoeyKlein.com/Speaking to learn more about booking Joey to speak.

THE INNER MATRIX

LEVERAGING THE ART & SCIENCE OF PERSONAL MASTERY TO CREATE REAL LIFE RESULTS

Struggling to get the results you're striving for? Discover a powerful mind-science fusion to smash your goals and skyrocket your lifestyle.

Can't seem to bust through plateaus? Want to level up but keep falling down? Wish you could stop the self-sabotage? Founder and CEO of Inner Matrix Systems, Joey Klein has specialized for over twenty years in helping high-achievers master the inner game of performance. Now he's here to share his proprietary methods to help you maximize your outcomes and reap sustainable rewards.

The Inner Matrix: Leveraging the Art & Science of Personal Mastery to Create Real Life Results is a comprehensive program to realign your emotional, mental, and physical states to support the achievement of down-to-earth objectives. Using Klein's heavily researched and carefully developed techniques, exercises, and on-the-ground examples, you'll easily open up new vistas of accomplishments. And by focusing on eliminating stress, mastering your emotions, and aiming for high-impact results, your most sought-after dreams will soon be right at your fingertips.

In The Inner Matrix, you'll discover:

- A simple, practical approach to managing your emotions, thought strategies, and nervous system to channel success

- Ways to develop fulfillment, peace, and inspiration

- How to create the neurological alignment needed to achieve any outcome you desire

- Methods for training yourself to design a rich and meaningful life

- Case studies, scientific references, expert insights, and much, much more!

The Inner Matrix is the only manual you need to break through any barrier and knock your goals out of the park. If you like powerful concepts, logical frameworks to follow, and direct instructions that actually work, then you'll love Joey Klein's motivational masterpiece.

Visit InnerMatrix.com to get your copy.

ABOUT THE AUTHOR

Joey Klein is a Transformation and Mastery Expert, Author, Speaker, and the Founder & CEO of Inner Matrix Systems, a personal mastery training system for high achievers. He is the author of *The Inner Matrix: Leveraging the Art & Science of Personal Mastery to Create Real Life Results* and *Relationship Alchemy: A Practical Guide to Getting Along Well With Others*.

After crawling out of the ditch of a hard-partying lifestyle that culminated in a near-death experience at 19 years old, Joey set out on a journey to find peace and joy for himself. He became obsessed with figuring out how to make instant transformation possible, a quest which took him all over the world to study different traditional disciplines like meditation, martial arts, and spiritual traditions. Upon his return, he studied with expert psychologists and neuroscientists, ultimately leading him to create his proprietary Inner Matrix Method. While instant transformation is possible, Joey's enduring passion is training mastery inside himself and his clients to truly live the life that's possible for each one of us.

Since starting Inner Matrix Systems in 2002, Joey has trained over 84,000 individuals worldwide, including executives from Fortune 500 companies, entrepreneurs, and professional athletes to ensure their vision is not only enduring but actually creates the fulfillment and impact they desire.

As a result of his research, training, and experience, Joey has long been considered an expert on the inner game of performance and is passionate about supporting his clients to live their life all-out with fulfillment and purpose. He embodies this passion through his core values of Excellence, Ownership, Mastery, Integrity, and Results.

Among his clients, Joey has a reputation of fixing un-fixable problems, removing the obstacles that keep them from the life of their dreams, and making himself responsible for their desired outcome until it's fulfilled. He puts himself directly in the trenches with every client to ensure they achieve the results they're looking for. His methods are direct, comprehensive, and proven to produce the desired outcome every time.

Joey currently lives in Colorado and enjoys hiking, skiing, and cycling to fulfill his desire for fun and adventure.

www.ingramcontent.com/pod-product-compliance
Lightning Source LLC
Chambersburg PA
CBHW020539030426
42337CB00013B/912